New York Times Bestselling Author

Sarah Burleton

WHY ME?

Cover created by JT Net Inc.

ISBN: 1470052555
ISBN-13: 978-1470052553

Prologue

I was born in Melrose Park, Illinois, on a cold day in November 1978 to a young woman not ready or willing to have a child. I would be told later in life that I was supposed to be an abortion, but the hospital called my grandma instead of my mother to give her news of my pregnancy; thus, my mother was "forced" to have me. Looking back now, I think I spent my childhood paying the price for a hospital nurse dialing the wrong number.

I wrote this book after debating over it for a decade. I didn't want to insult anyone or make anyone mad by telling my story—I was worried about how my mother would feel about it if she read it and how my sister would feel. But in the end, I feel compelled to share my story with others. I know that there are other abused kids out there, kids who on the outside may just seem weird or who maybe don't have the best haircut or the best clothes, who are facing the same teasing at school and torture at home that I faced.

Abuse for me was something that happened on a daily basis. It might have been a hair-pulling, a punch to the kidneys, a kick down the stairs, or Mom's other favorite activity: name-calling. Over the years I have been called Thunder Thighs, Nigger Lips, Kidney Kate (because I had kidney problems when I was younger), and Anorexic Annie, just to name a few. I've been beaten with brooms, whips, extension cords, belts—basically, if it was in arm's reach, I was getting hit with it. I spent nights awake in a bathroom, hovered over a tray table writing *I will not lie* until the wee hours of the morning, and my hand would cramp up so badly I couldn't move it the next day. I never fully understood why I was beaten so much. Some days it was because I didn't do a chore properly; other days it was because I took too long in the bathroom. A lot of the time, after my sister was born, it was because Mom thought I was being mean to my sister.

Another reason I avoided writing this book for so long was that I didn't want to play the victim. I wanted to just suck it up, take my knocks, and learn from my experience. Yet I don't believe I am playing the victim in this book. If anything, I am releasing years of hurt and anger that I have been harboring.

I had a tough time figuring out exactly what to include in the book. Should I detail every single abusive experience I had growing up? That seemed silly and outlandish. What seemed right for me, and I hope will feel right for readers of this book, was to write about what first popped into my head when I thought of my childhood.

What childhood events and experiences do you remember the most? When many people think about growing up, they remember events and experiences such as birthday parties (and even I can say that was one thing my mother did—give me great birthdays), sleepovers, and family times together. But when I looked back, seriously sat down and looked back on my childhood, certain traumatic experiences came to mind. These are experiences I can never block out and have never forgotten. These are the experiences that I believe shaped me into the person I am today. These are the experiences I wanted to write about.

I want readers of this book to know that I've been there and I'm still alive and I'm happy and there IS light at the end of the tunnel. No matter how dark it may seem some nights when you are lying in bed, sniffling because you have just been beaten again, it WILL get better. Abuse is not acceptable in any form, and if you are being physically or mentally abused, please tell someone—a friend, relative, teacher or neighbor. It's not right! You deserve better!

Dedicated to Aron, Evan, and Gage
Thank you for loving me so much.

Chapter 1

Where were you that day?

Do you remember where you were the day the space shuttle *Challenger* exploded? I will never forget. I was sitting in my first-grade classroom trying not to pee my pants. You see, I had already been to the bathroom three times that day, and Mrs. Slagle had told me that I was not allowed to go anymore, I was just messing around. To my mind, that was absolutely absurd.

"How does she know how many times I have to pee? I drank two huge glasses of juice this morning!"

Two glasses was a lot of juice, and Mrs. Slagle was a brilliant teacher. She should have realized that a little girl's bladder couldn't hold that much! But I couldn't tell Mrs. Slagle that I had drunk so much juice because then I would have had to explain why.

I had been bad again that morning. I didn't finish my oatmeal "because it tastes like gluc," and Mom got mad. Sometimes when Mom got mad she would just yell and scream and push me around a little bit. But a lot of the time when Mom got mad things went very, very badly for me. This morning was one of those mornings.

I had gotten up on the wrong side of the bed that morning. I was dreading school because Mom had just cut my hair . . . again. This time she had not only cut my hair, she had Ogilvie-permed it, and now I looked like a French poodle. Mom wasn't the best at perms. She rolled the rollers so tight that the little needles cut into my scalp, and she layered on the stinky perm solution so thick that it dripped down my face and left red marks wherever it touched.

I knew the kids at school would make fun of my hair that day. I already got teased on a daily basis because my family was poor. We didn't live in a cardboard box or beg for food, but we were poor enough that, for some reason, the local paper had done a cover story (with a full-color picture!) about how poor my family was and how we were struggling in the current economy. That newspaper article provided the kids at school with enough ammunition and jokes aimed at me to last until middle school.

"This hair is going to really get them going today," I thought to myself as I looked in the mirror that morning. I wrapped my bath towel around my head and swirled around, pretending that I had beautiful, cascading black hair that streamed all the way down my back. As I swirled, I imagined myself dancing in a ballroom in a beautiful blue gown.

"SARAH!"

I jumped and snapped out of my daydream. Mom was at my bedroom door, and she had the "look." It was the same look people get when they have just stepped in dog droppings—a combination of disgust and sickness.

"What the hell are you doing in here?"

I quickly pulled the towel from my head and acted like I was getting dressed. "Nothing, Mom. I'm getting ready for school."

Mom looked at me and didn't say anything for a moment. It was as if she was waiting for me to say or do something wrong. A knot grew in my stomach.

"Quit messing around," said Mom. "Come out and eat. It's oatmeal."

"Awwwww . . . oatmeal? Come on!"

Mom's eyes seemed to glaze over. In two swift steps she was at my side. She grabbed me by my newly permed hair and dragged me out of my room. The pain was excruciating; my scalp was raw from the perm the night before, and my hair was still wet from my shower. I screamed and cried as Mom pulled me down the hallway, but fighting only made my head hurt worse.

"Shut up!" Mom yelled. "Do you want the whole building to hear you? I'm sick of you! I didn't want you in the first place!"

"I didn't want you in the first place" was a phrase I heard often. For a long time, I didn't understand what Mom was saying because the idea that a mother wouldn't want a child was foreign to me.

Mom dragged me to the dining room, where an extremely unappetizing bowl of gray oatmeal sat. I should have been grateful; a lot of people would absolutely love a bowl of hot oatmeal in the morning. Unfortunately, I am not one of those people. I sat down, sniffing and sobbing, and picked at the bowl of oatmeal.

"Sarah, I'm not going to tell you again. Eat your oatmeal! You have school in half an hour." Mom's voice had gone from angry to pleading, but I was already too upset to buy into her up-and-down games.

"I DON'T WANT OATMEAL!" I yelled. Before the words even left my mouth, I knew they were a mistake. But I didn't care; I was already dreading going to school and figured I had nothing to lose.

"You bitch!" Mom hissed. Again, she was at my side in two large steps. She grabbed me by the hair and dragged me into the kitchen. "Sit down!" she snapped, gesturing at a small stool next to the cabinet. I sat down and readied myself. I knew what was coming.

Mom reached into the cabinet under the sink and pulled out the Ajax liquid dish soap. "Open your mouth!" she ordered. I tipped my head back and plugged my nose. "No, leave your nose unplugged! I want you to taste it!" Mom opened the cap and poured what seemed like a cup of soap into my mouth. "Now sit there and hold that!"

One of my favorite movies was *A Christmas Story*. I loved the scene where Ralphie got in trouble for using a swear word and got his mouth washed out with soap. The square red block of soap going into his mouth looked like the most horrible thing anyone could ever taste. So whenever Mom put soap in my mouth, I flashed to this scene from the movie. It made me laugh a little on the inside and feel better as I thought of someone else getting soap put in his mouth. But I imagined that liquid soap must actually be worse than bar soap, because I always swallowed a lot of it as I sat there and tried to hold it in my mouth. My gag reflex would kick in, but if I spit the soap out, Mom would start all over again.

Finally, Mom brought over a bowl and told me to spit the soap out of my mouth. I got up and rushed to the sink to rinse my mouth out, but Mom grabbed me by the arm. "Not in my kitchen sink, you idiot! In the bathroom!"

I ran to the bathroom with tears streaming down my face and soap bubbling out of my mouth. I stuck my face under the faucet and let the water stream into my mouth. I spit and spit for what seemed like an hour, but I couldn't get the soapy taste to go away. Then I heard my mother calling, "Sarah! Come here and drink some juice! You don't have time to eat now!"

I wiped my face clean, spit one more time, and went out to the kitchen, where Mom was standing with a glass of orange juice. I downed the juice in three large gulps and held the glass out for more. Mom smiled at me and opened the fridge to get out the juice and pour me another cup. I immediately felt better. I thought that by her little smile, Mom had forgiven me, and everything was OK now. "Thanks, Mom!" I said.

"Mmm-hmm," Mom said as she handed me my second glass of orange juice.

I downed that glass in two gulps and smiled at Mom as I handed the glass back. "That was good!" I said.

"Get your bag and get out the door to school," Mom replied. She turned her back and went to the sink to wash the cup I had just dirtied.

So this was why I had to pee so bad and had already gone to the bathroom three times that day. But I couldn't tell my teacher why I had to pee. Mrs. Slagle always asked a lot of questions when I told a story. If I said I had to pee because I had had two huge glasses of orange juice that morning, then Mrs. Slagle would want to know why I had drunk so much juice. The stories I made up about bruises on my neck or cuts on my arms usually involved falling down stairs or walking clumsily into door frames, but I could tell that Mrs. Slagle didn't always believe me. Sometimes I tried more glorious adventure stories. But now I just wasn't up to spinning a tale about being stranded in a desert the night before and becoming so dehydrated that I couldn't live without two huge glasses of orange juice this morning.

So I was sitting in the back of the room wiggling like a worm on a fishhook, trying to hold my legs together until the bell rang and I could go to the bathroom, when the second-grade teacher ran into the room wheeling a large television.

"Ladies and gentlemen! Quiet, please!" Mrs. Slagle clapped her thin hands together and repositioned the large black glasses on her nose. "Today is the day the *Challenger* takes off into space! Remember how we talked about the teacher on this flight, Christa McAuliffe? We are going to see her and the other astronauts launch into space in about five minutes, right here on television!"

Of course I remembered our discussions about the space shuttle. Until my class started learning about the *Challenger* flight, I had known nothing of outer space. The whole concept of other worlds, deep space, stars, planets, and galaxies was amazing to me. The prospect of actually seeing a space shuttle take off into space with a teacher on board was almost too much!

As Mrs. Slagle and the second-grade teacher busied themselves plugging in the television, finding the right channel, and adjusting the rabbit-ear antenna, I tried to figure out how I was going to survive another five minutes without going to the bathroom. There was no way. I had to make a run for it. I began to slide down out of my chair. I was going to crawl out of the room, dash across the hall to the bathroom, and make it back before Mrs. Slagle had even turned around. The plan seemed brilliant, but then . . .

Just as I slid out of my chair, I heard, "Sarah! That's it! Come up here and get your pass to the principal's office!" I hung my head. Getting sent to the principal's office meant a phone call home. My day had just gotten worse.

I quickly walked up to Mrs. Slagle's desk, where my pass to the principal's office was waiting. The note said, "Trying to sneak out of classroom." But, to my surprise, Mrs. Slagle had not marked the "Call home to parents" box! "Awesome!" I thought to myself.

Mrs. Slagle peered over her glasses at me as she handed me the note. "Maybe it would be a good idea if you stopped in the bathroom on your way to the office," she said. I grinned at her and ran out of the room.

So that's where I was the day the *Challenger* exploded. I was sitting in the principal's office, watching the school administrators come out of their offices sobbing and shaking their heads in utter disbelief.

When I walked home that afternoon, I tried desperately to find something good to grasp onto for the day, anything positive to get me through the night. I thought about the astronauts who had been so excited and happy to wake up that morning, and how sad their families must be now that they were gone forever. "My life isn't that bad," I thought. "At least I wasn't on that shuttle."

I walked up to my apartment door and opened it. There stood my mother with the bowl of oatmeal from that morning and a smile on her face.

Chapter 2

Rebecca's birthday

I loved birthdays. My birthday was one time during the year that I was made to feel like a princess and one of the few times that my mother was actually nice to me all day long. As a child, my birthday celebrations had included big family get-togethers, Pizza Hut pizza-making parties, and smaller family parties. For some reason, birthdays were very important to Mom, and she would become consumed with trying to make bigger and better birthday parties every year. She almost looked forward to birthdays more than I did.

There was no better way to spend a birthday morning than l in Mrs. Beamish's 3rd grade clasroom. The birthday student would get a special decorated chair for the day, wear a crown on his or her head, and be leader in every line for the entire day! The principal would even get on the loudspeaker and wish the student a happy birthday—so the entire school would know about it!

Today was Rebecca's birthday. Rebecca was a "sort-of" friend of mine. She acted like my friend outside of the school walls, but during the school day she would pick on me all the time. This didn't bother me too much, though, because I thought Rebecca was the most beautiful girl in the school and I loved spending as much time with her as I could.

Rebecca had the life that I dreamed of. She had a big house, two dogs, and a really nice mom and dad. I would sit in Rebecca's house sometimes and watch in amazement as

Rebecca's mom hugged and kissed her and combed the tangles out of her long hair.

"That family is just weird!" my mom would say. "They're a little too touchy-feely for my liking." But I didn't think their behavior was weird. To me, it looked right.

I was on my way to school that morning when I heard Rebecca's sing-song voice call out "Sarah! Wait for me!" I turned around and saw Rebecca was running up behind me, wearing the prettiest white dress with pink flowers lining the hem. Her mother had curled her hair that morning and put a shiny silver tiara at the top that glistened in the sunlight. At that moment, I felt a pang of jealousy in my stomach. For the first time, I hated Rebecca, hated her for having a mother who let her have long hair, hated her for wearing such a pretty dress and such a pretty sparkly thing in her hair.

"Aren't you going to wish me a happy birthday?" Rebecca asked breathlessly.

"That's right!" I exclaimed. "Happy Birthday!"

"Thanks!" said Rebecca. "I had such a good morning with my mom and dad! They made me orange French toast and hot cocoa . . . mmmmm, my favorites!"

I hadn't had the best morning with my mother and stepfather, so the last thing I wanted to hear was how great someone else's morning had been—but I plastered on a fake smile and said, "Wow! That sounds so good!"

"I know! Then tonight we're having a party and cake and . . ." Rebecca stopped mid-sentence as we approached the school playground. She ran off, leaving me in the dust of her Nancy Janes. That was our friendship, outside of school grounds only!

I walked into our classroom early and saw that Rebecca's chair was already decorated and a birthday crown was waiting on her desk. Mrs. Beamish was sitting at her big desk at the front of the room, grading papers from the day before.

"Sarah, why are you in here so early?" she asked. "Go outside and play with your friends."

I desperately wanted to say, "I'm having a bad day and I want to just sit in here and get this day over with," but I didn't want to explain why I was having a bad day. So I turned around and went back out to playground. I sat down on an empty swing and watched as all the kids swarmed around Rebecca, glorifying her on her special day.

"It's not fair," I thought to myself. I wanted it to be my birthday. I wanted today to be a day when Mom spoiled me and the kids at school were nice to me and it was MY special day for once.

The longer I sat and stewed, the angrier I got. Finally, after what seemed like a million years, the first bell of the day rang. "Nice hair, Poodle," said one of my classmates as we entered the building. That was the last straw. I stopped dead in my tracks, turned around, and punched the little boy who had made the poodle remark as hard as I could. The hallway went quiet, and everyone turned around and stared at me.

I felt shocked at what I'd done, but my small fist was still curled up, ready for round two. The little boy who had borne the brunt of my wrath was standing there with tears streaming down his face. I faintly whispered "I'm sorry" before I felt the enormous hands of the principal, Mr. Scott, on my shoulders and was led down to his office.

"Sarah," he said quietly, "you know better than to hit. I'm giving you a detention before school tomorrow."

My heart sank. The detention didn't bother me, but taking the dreaded pink slip home to my mother was going to be horrible. I watched as Mr. Scott filled out the pink slip, my mind racing. "Maybe I can fake Mom's signature; maybe I can run away . . ." Ideas flooded my head on how to avoid punishment for this, but none of them were any good. I would just have to go home after school and face whatever happened.

I spent the rest of the day sulking in the back of the classroom, the pit in my stomach growing while everyone fawned over Rebecca and whispered and talked about me. When the last bell finally rang at 3:05, I waited until everyone had left the classroom and then approached her teacher, Mrs. Beamish. "I'm sorry for hitting Michael," I said in a soft voice, looking up with eyes pleading her to please make this pink slip go away.

Mrs. Beamish said, "I'm glad you're sorry, Sarah, but you have to take responsibility for your actions, honey!"

My eyes welled up with tears, and I nodded my head and turned around. Just as I was about to leave the room, Mrs. Beamish said, "Just remember, Sarah, tomorrow is another day, a fresh start."

For some reason, those words resonated in my mind and I felt a little better. Tomorrow would be a new day, a fresh start, and no matter what happened when I got home that afternoon, I would wake up tomorrow to a new day.

I walked home twice as slowly as usual. Rebecca didn't walk home with me that day; she was busy with her school friends, talking about how great her party was going to be that night. Oh, how I wished today was my birthday and I was the one looking forward to cake and presents and family time!

I approached our apartment building, and my feet turned into lead. They didn't want to go in, and who could blame them? Even my feet knew that what waited for me behind the door of our apartment couldn't be good.

I finally opened the apartment door. Mom was vacuuming the living room for what was probably the fifth or sixth time that day. I took off my shoes and walked into the living room. Mom turned off the vacuum.

"So, I heard you had a bad day at school today," she said in a calm voice.

The voice threw me off; this was not my mother's normal reaction. I felt a bit calmer.

"I hit Michael," I said meekly.

"Why?" Mom asked.

"I wanted it to be my birthday," I replied.

"We'll talk about this when your father gets home," Mom said, and she turned the vacuum back on and continued cleaning.

I turned around and went to my room, relieved by the lack of reaction from Mom but also confused about why she wasn't hitting or screaming at me right now. The comment Mom had made about my father made me bristle.

The man Mom was referring to wasn't my father; in fact, I wasn't even sure who my biological father really was. This man, my stepfather, was someone Mom had met while waitressing. After a whirlwind romance, they were married and I was told to call him Dad. I had never felt comfortable around my stepdad. I didn't know him well; he had just appeared out of the blue one day. While he hadn't put his hands on me yet, he never argued with Mom or stopped her from hitting me all the time. For this reason, I didn't trust my stepfather and never would.

I spent the rest of the afternoon in my bedroom. As the minutes and hours ticked away, the pit in my stomach grew and grew. Something was wrong. Mom was never this calm. Or maybe something was right, and I was getting a fresh start like Mrs. Beamish had said. Maybe everything was going to be OK.

Finally I heard my stepdad's blue drywall truck pull up in front of the apartment building. My entire body started trembling. The room seemed to close in on me, and I lay down on the bed with my eyes squeezed shut. Then I heard my mother's voice.

"Sarah, come out and eat dinner. Your father is home."

I opened the door to my room and walked into the tiny apartment dining room where my mother and stepdad were waiting. Tonight we were having stuffed green peppers, my favorite meal in the entire world! Maybe this day was going to end up OK! Why would Mom go to the effort of making my favorite dinner if I was in trouble? I sat down happily in my seat at the table and began to dig into my first green pepper.

"So I heard you had a bad day today, Sarah," my stepdad said.

"I hit Michael, and I have a detention tomorrow morning," I replied matter-of-factly, thinking that all was forgiven and I could dare to be a bit bold.

My mom and stepdad looked at each other and continued to eat. The meal continued in silence. The silence lasted until the dishes were done and I was sitting in front of the television.

Then my stepdad said in a quiet voice, "Sarah, go into our bedroom."

I got up from my seat in the living room and went back to Mom's bedroom, which was pretty stark. The bed was neatly made, and there was a dresser on the far wall with a large mirror. When you sat on the bed, you could see yourself perfectly in the mirror, so I sat on the bed and watched myself bounce up and down in the mirror until my stepdad entered the room.

"'Take your pants off, Sarah," he said, and he started to undo the belt on his work pants.

I immediately curled up into a ball and started crying. "What are you going to do to me?" I cried out.

"SHUT UP AND DO AS YOUR FATHER ASKS!" Mom bellowed from the kitchen.

With tears streaming down my face, I slowly unbuttoned my pants, took them off, and laid them on the floor. "Pull your underwear down," my stepdad instructed. I did so and then sat down on the bed, completely naked from the waist down and humiliated and scared at the same time.

"Turn over" was the next calm instruction from my stepdad. Confused, I remained seated and turned my back to him on the bed. "No, face down," he said.

I buried my face in my mother's pillow, smelling the faint scent of her perfume and shampoo. Then I turned my head and looked at myself in the mirror on the dresser. I couldn't see my stepfather, but I heard the belt snap in his hands.

"CRACK!" My naked rear end was immediately on fire. The hard leather belt had come cracking down on me with such force that I thought something had broken in my body. I screamed out in pain, and Mom came running into the room and put her hand over my mouth.

My stepdad raised the belt again. I could see the reflection of his hand in the mirror as it started to come down, and I squirmed and fought my mother's hand holding me down. Snot started dripping out of my nose. Mom took her hand away in disgust and smacked me on the side of the head before she wiped her hand on my shirt.

"CRACK!" The belt came down again. Now my rear end felt like it was bleeding. I had wiggled too much, and that belt strike had hit me not only on the behind, but also across the backs of my legs. The pain was almost too much to bear. Mom resumed her grip on my mouth.

"A detention, huh? This will teach you to get a detention, you little loser!"

"CRACK, CRACK, CRACK!" After three more strikes with the belt, my stepdad left the room. Mom got up and followed him, leaving me motionless and shaking on the bed. I didn't dare cry out or leave the room; my survival instincts said to just lie there and hope it was over.

Soon my mom and stepdad reentered their bedroom with two cold, wet washcloths. "Jesus Christ, we left marks," my stepdad said to my mom. I remained motionless as they almost lovingly covered the welts on my rear end and legs with the cold rags.

Eventually one of them told me to go to bed; then, finally, I was out of that room and away from them. My emotions were running wild; I didn't know up from down or left from right. Lying on my stomach, I sobbed into my pillow. My legs were on fire and my rear end was numb. I felt betrayed. The night, which I had thought was going to be good, had turned into another night of terror.

I gritted my teeth and bit down on my pillow to avoid screaming out in anger. Then my mind went to Rebecca and how happy she must be at that moment with her family. She was probably getting presents and hugs and kisses while I lay on the bed covered in welts.

"Why does it have to be me?" I sobbed. "What did I do to deserve this?" Then I remembered. "I got a detention." Immediately I felt deep remorse for hitting Michael. I had made him hurt like I was hurting now. I understood why I'd gotten in trouble and wanted nothing more than to run to Michael's house and apologize for being so mean.

As I drifted off to sleep, I imagined that the next day was my birthday. I imagined waking up to a French toast and hot cocoa breakfast, and Mom dressing me up and combing my hair. I imagined a room full of friends and family, all there for me, happy for me, and loving me.

"Happy Birthday, Rebecca," I said quietly.

= Chapter 3 =

We named the goat Indiana!

Less than a year after they were married, my mother and stepfather had a child of their own, a daughter named Emily. I loved Emily, but I always felt jealous of her in a way. Mom was so nice to Emily, really kind and caring at times. Mom would get mad at me and hold Emily tight and say, "Well, at least I have one good daughter that I love so, SO much!" I began to grow quite resentful of Emily and spent a lot of time distancing myself from her.

A few months after the belt incident, I came home from school to find Mom sitting with Emily at the kitchen table. Mom was on the phone, and there was a newspaper open on the kitchen table. I glanced over Mom's shoulder and saw that the paper was open to the real estate section and Mom had a lot of places circled.

"What's going on, Mom?" I asked.

"We're moving," Mom said. "Some damn Mexicans are moving in next door, and we are out of here."

Whether that was the truth or not, I was taken aback by my mother's surprise announcement. Since Emily had been born, things had gotten worse for me at home but better at school. I had made a very good friend named Debbie, and we spent all our time together. I had met Debbie while I was wandering around the neighborhood one day. A little girl with a hula hoop called me over, and we spent the next two hours hula-hooping and dancing to our hearts' content. Since that day, we had been inseparable.

Debbie never made fun of me like the other kids did. I confided in Debbie the things that went on at home and didn't spare details about the numerous beatings and other punishments I received. My mom and stepdad had moved on from the belt beatings to other weird forms of punishment. They still relied on the old liquid soap standby, but Mom moved on from slapping and whipping to choking and punching. There were many times that I wasn't allowed to go to school because of fingernail marks and bruises around my neck. Mom had also purchased a horse right after Emily was born, and she bought snappy little riding crops that she enjoyed smacking me around with. Talking to Debbie was my release—I could confide in her without worrying about someone calling the authorities on my mom and stepdad.

My eyes welled up with tears and I said to Mom, "What do you mean we're moving? What about my friends? Where are we going?" The questions wouldn't stop pouring out of my mouth.

Emily was starting to get fussy, and Mom picked her up. "Don't ask me questions I don't know the answer to," she replied. "When we know—you will know."

"Can I go to Debbie's now?" I inquired. I had to get out of the house. I had to talk to Debbie and figure out a way that we could stay friends forever. Maybe I could live in Debbie's basement and sleep on the pool table or something, or maybe we could pitch a tent in her backyard and just stay there.

"I don't care what you do. Just be back at 4:00 to set the table and get ready for dinner."

Mom had barely gotten the words out of her mouth when I was tearing out the door, running down the street, and cutting through backyards to get to Debbie's house as soon as possible. It had been so hard for me to make a friend like Debbie; the prospect of starting over and finding someone else I could trust so completely scared me to death.

Bang, bang, bang! I pounded on Debbie's front door. A few seconds later, Debbie was there, eating a bag of Doritos.

"What's wrong?" she asked with a worried look on her face.

I unloaded on her. I told Debbie that my family was moving, but I didn't know where and I didn't know when. All I knew was that it was inevitable—and that I couldn't live without Debbie. If I didn't have someone to talk to, I was sure I would lose my mind. Debbie cut me off and said, "You aren't moved yet! Come on downstairs and let's play dress-up."

Dress-up was our favorite game. Downstairs in Debbie's basement were what seemed like thousands upon thousands of old dresses, shoes, and pieces of costume jewelry. I never wondered where they came from or why they were there. All I knew was that while I was at Debbie's, I could be anything I wanted to be. Sometimes I pretended to be a beautiful princess like Cinderella, and other times I was a famous singer.

For the next 45 minutes, Debbie and I played to our hearts' content. Then I heard the grandfather clock in Debbie's living room strike four o'clock. "Oh, shoot—I have to go set the table for dinner," I said.

Debbie grabbed my hand. "I'll see you tomorrow, Sarah, I promise."

But I never saw Debbie again. Mom wasn't kidding about moving; we were packed up and moved out so fast it almost made my head spin. Mom kept me home from school to help pack up the house, and we moved out in less than a week.

I will never forget pulling up to the farmhouse for the first time. It had taken over two hours of driving to get there, followed by what seemed like an hour of driving down the long driveway, but finally my stepdad stopped the truck. I looked out the window and got my first glimpse of our new home. It was a large white house in the middle of two enormous farm fields. I had been in a barn before because of my mother's interest in horses, but I had never been on a farm. There were about five barns on the property, most of which were full of old, rusty farm equipment and looked like they were going to fall down at any second. The house looked old and creaky, with no front porch steps and paint peeling off the sides. I could have made up a year's worth of ghost stories to tell Debbie just based on my first impressions, but the thought that popped into my mind was "Oh, my God— there's no one around to hear me scream."

It wasn't long before Mom had the farm filled up with all the animals she had ever wanted. We had two horses, a coop full of chickens, and a number of geese and goats that wandered around in the pasture. With these animals came a lot of work. Every morning at five o'clock, rain or shine, snow or sleet, I was up hauling buckets of water to the horse troughs, mucking out stalls, and cleaning up the pasture. I didn't mind the work, and I enjoyed spending time with the animals. They listened to me talk and vent about Mom, and the big quarter horse Buddy was a solid shoulder to cry on when I needed it the most. In a way, the farm animals were my replacement for Debbie.

When I was about 10 years old I fell in love with Indiana Jones. I had seen my first Indiana Jones movie and was immediately lovestruck by this man in leather saving the damsel in distress from the dangerous Nazis. I adorned my room with Indiana Jones posters and decorated my notebooks with *I love Indy*. Right around this time, Mom and Richard bought me my own goat. It was a sickly, ugly little thing, but it was mine and that was all I cared about. I named the goat Indy, after my beloved Indiana Jones. Every morning when I went out to do the chores, Indy was waiting at the electric fence, bleating for me and ready to chase me around the pasture. Every afternoon when I got off the school bus, Indy would be waiting for me again. When I went riding, he would follow behind the horse. Indy might have been just a goat to most people, but to me, alone in the middle of a cornfield, he was one of my best friends.

Although Mom had purchased the goat for me, she reminded me every day how much she hated that goat, how it ate her flowers and destroyed things in her garden. I would quickly defend Indy, using the argument "Well, he's a goat! What do you expect?"

Mom's response was to go out and buy a BB gun. She shot it at Indy during the day while I was at school. I knew in my heart that it was only a matter of time before Mom really hurt Indy or got rid of him, so every morning I would get on my knees and beg Indy to be good and stay in the pasture.

Indy would look up at me with his big eyes like he understood, but I could also see the glint in his eyes as he surveyed the yard around the farmhouse and decided what he was going to eat that day. And every day when I came home from school, Mom was at the door with the BB gun, aiming it and shooting at Indy when he got near.

One morning, I had done my chores, given Indy his pep talk, and boarded the bus to school. Then I looked out the bus window and saw Mom pumping up the BB gun. My heart sank. "Indy, stay in the pasture today, PLEASE!" I whispered. As the bus pulled away, I saw Mom step outside and head toward the pasture.

The entire day was a blur. I couldn't stop thinking about Indy and wondering if he was OK. Usually, Mom would just hit him a few times in the hindquarters and he would go away. But this morning something had been different with Mom. She had smacked me around a few times for not bringing down enough hay bales for the horses and paced through the kitchen muttering to herself about how much she hated me and her entire life. "Stick me out here on this goddamn farm with this little bitch? Not if I can help it," she had muttered. So I knew Mom was not in the best mood, and without me there to knock around, she would turn to the next best thing, my animal.

Finally, the school day ended and I boarded the big yellow bus to head home. After an excruciatingly long ride, the bus finally came to a halt at the foot of our driveway. I hurried off the bus and took a quick survey of the pasture. Indy was nowhere to be seen, but everything else looked normal. I walked up the long gravel driveway and went through the side door into the kitchen. Mom was in there, kneading bread dough and humming a tune that I had never heard before.

"Smells good in here, Mom!" I said cautiously.

"It does smell yummy, doesn't it? Why don't you go change and take care of the animals before dinner?"

Everything seemed normal, so I did as I was asked. I changed into my farm clothes, grabbed my work gloves, and headed down to the pasture. As I approached the barn that housed the horses and the goats, I heard a strange sound, like a whimpering cat

"Indy!" I called out. It was rare for Indy to not be at my side by now, nosing me around and head-butting me. Something was amiss.

I opened the barn door and couldn't believe my eyes. There lay Indy, covered in blood, in the corner of his pen. He was still alive, but it was obvious that Mom had spent the entire day shooting him full of BBs. I picked up Indy's head and noticed that several BBs had been shot directly into it, as if Mom had pressed the gun barrel up against his head and pulled the trigger until the clip ran out.

I tried to count how many BBs Indy had been shot with, but there were too many to count. Blood was pouring out of what seemed like every part of his body. Indy looked up at me as if to say, "I'm sorry!" I held his head gingerly and sobbed. I don't know how long I sat there holding Indy in my arms, but when my tears finally stopped for a second and I could see clearly, Indy had died in my arms.

I felt a rage like I had never felt before in my life. Sure, I had gotten angry over the years after a night of beatings, but this was different. And Mom, standing in the kitchen humming like she'd just had the best day ever, was too much to bear.

I laid Indy's head gently on the straw in his pen, wiped my eyes, and stood up. I wanted to hit something, hit something of Mom's that would make her hurt like I was hurting. I curled up my fist and went looking for something to destroy. When

I walked out of the barn, the first thing I saw was Buddy, my mother's horse. Mom loved Buddy more than she loved any human being. She cuddled with that horse, slept with him when he was sick, brushed and primped him every day. The farmhouse was decorated with show ribbons she had won with Buddy and pictures of them together. It was impossible not to notice how much Mom loved that horse.

Without thinking, I marched up to Buddy with my fist curled. Buddy picked up his head from grazing and looked at me inquisitively, as if to say, "Are you bringing me a treat?" I only saw a blur of brown and black as I began punching Buddy anywhere I could reach. I kept punching until he ran away to the opposite side of the pasture.

Mom came tearing out of the house, eyes blazing and oven mitts still on her hands. She ran into the pasture and pushed me down onto the ground.

"What the fuck is wrong with you, you piece of shit? You goddamn no-good piece of shit!" This tirade of name-calling was nothing new to me—in fact, the moment Mom opened her mouth, I tuned her out. I remained on the ground, trying to dodge Mom's boots kicking me in the side and covering my head with my hands to protect it from the blows coming from all directions.

"Mommy!" I heard. Emily was at the kitchen door, looking out into the pasture. Mom stopped kicking me long enough to turn and look at her, giving me the opportunity to roll as far away from her as possible before she turned back around.

When Mom turned back to me, she spoke through gritted teeth. "I'm going to kill you! You know that, right?" she said. "Get your fat ass in the house, NOW!"

Mom stepped aside so I could walk to the house in front of her. I got up and scurried around her, walking as fast as possible toward the electric fence surrounding the pasture. In my haste to get to Indy, I had forgotten to switch the electric fence off, but I didn't remember this. Mom did, though.

In the blink of an eye, Mom ran up behind me and pushed me into the fence. Instinctively, I reached out my arms to stop my fall and ended up grabbing the live fence. My hands clamped around the thin wires, and my body collapsed to the ground as the electricity coursed through it. I opened my eyes and saw my mother standing over me with the strangest smile on her face. "Oh, my God, I'm going to die!" I thought in panic.

Through the grace of God—or maybe with the help of Mom—I pried my hands free from that electric fence. Then I just lay on the ground, looking up at the sky and shaking. I kept seeing Indy's face looking up at me, and rage seethed in my heart.

Mom looked down and said, "I need to get inside to my daughter. Get your ass up!" So I got up, crawled under the electric fence, and wobbled into the house, all the while fighting the urge to turn around and shove Mom's face into a steaming pile of her beloved Buddy's manure.

While I sat on the pull-out couch in my room, trying to recover emotionally and physically from the day's events, Mom and Emily happily stood in the kitchen making homemade bread for dinner. Eventually I cried myself to sleep. I missed dinner that night, but I didn't care—at least I was left alone to mourn the loss of my best friend on the farm.

The next day when I got up to do my morning chores, I saw that my stepdad had thrown Indy's lifeless body behind the barn. Flies were swarming around it, feasting on every hole Mom had put into Indy's body the previous day. I went to the tool shed, got a shovel, and buried my best friend under a tree behind the horse barn. I even carved a little headstone out of a piece of bark and shoved it into the ground. For the first time in my life, I felt true hatred toward my mother.

= Chapter 4 =

Behind the pantry door

Life on the farm didn't get any easier for me after Indy died. School was nothing to talk about. I had no friends to speak of, and I lived too far out in the country to be involved in anything in town. School was just a place I went because I had to—and because it was a way to escape the house for six hours every day.

Mom was obviously losing her mind in the farmhouse. She didn't work, and my stepdad's job was a 45-minute drive away. Once Emily started going to school and Mom spent more and more time alone, the situation at home went from bad to worse.

One day when Emily and I got off the school bus, Mom was sitting in a chair in front of the pantry.

"What are you doing, Mom?" I asked.

"Nothing," she said. She got up quickly to check Emily's book bag and get her an after-school snack.

I walked toward the closed pantry door. As I got closer, a foul smell overwhelmed me. I put one hand on the pantry doorknob and covered my mouth and nose with the other hand, just to have some sort of fresh air entering my body. Then I slowly opened the pantry door.

Immediately I noticed a strange thing dangling from the ceiling. I flicked on the light and saw that it was one of the neighbors' cats. Mom had killed it and strung it up in the pantry. Although the cat was dead, terror shot through my veins. I stood there thinking that the cat was going to come back to life and claw my eyes out.

I couldn't speak; I couldn't move; I couldn't even breathe. I was in complete shock as the cat swayed back and forth from the ceiling. I couldn't even wrap my mind around this horror. I knew that I would never forget the sight of that cat or the awful smell emitting from the pantry.

Finally I turned and walked back into the kitchen, where Mom was fixing Emily a snack of bread and homemade apple butter and talking cheerfully with her about her day at school.

"Mom! Why did you kill that cat?" I asked in a shaky voice.

Mom didn't even answer; she just kept on making Emily's snack as if there was nothing strange about a dead cat hanging in the pantry. I glanced at Emily, who didn't seem to notice that there was a problem.

"Isn't it time for you to go out and do your chores?" Mom asked me.

I rushed out of the house and into the horse barn, where I took a quick survey of the animals to make sure no others were hurt. Then I ran around to the back of the barn and threw up my lunch from earlier in the day. I couldn't get the foul smell of dead cat out of my nose and throat. As I was kneeling there, wiping the vomit from my lips, another cat from the neighboring farm came over and rubbed against my leg.

"No, no! Run away! Get out of here! Don't let her see you!" I whispered in panic to the little tabby cat. The tabby cat looked at me and meowed, as if to say, "I'm OK! Don't worry about me!"

I picked up the cat and ran deep into the cornfield that separated our farmhouse from the neighbors'. "Get out of here! No one wants you here!" I said angrily, dropping the little cat. I didn't want this cat to meet the same fate as the one that was dangling from our pantry ceiling. The little cat looked at me, then turned and ran toward its home.

I slowly made my way back through the cornfield and took an extra long time doing my chores. The horses got extra hay and especially clean stalls, and the chicken coops were cleaned to perfection. I didn't want to go back into the house and smell death again. I stayed out in the pasture until my stepfather pulled into the driveway. After he had gone inside, I followed to see his reaction to what Mom had done that day.

"Sarah, get in here and hold this bag open." My stepfather was in the pantry. He had the dead cat in his hands and was gesturing toward a large, empty horse feed bag. I was terrified. Not only did I not want to see the cat again, I didn't want to be anywhere near it.

"No, Dad! I don't want to!" I sobbed.

"What the hell are you scared of? The cat is dead! It won't hurt you!"

"I don't want to!" I sobbed again.

"Jesus Christ, Sarah," said Richard, "just get your ass over here and hold the bag."

There was no point in arguing. I was going to have to hold that bag regardless of my feelings or my fear of the dead cat.

I walked over to my stepdad, picked up the bag, and opened it wide. Then I turned my head and squeezed my eyes shut so I wouldn't see the cat go into the bag. As Richard began to put the dead cat into the bag, it rubbed against my hands. I cried out and backed away, dropping the bag.

"Goddamn it, Sarah! What the hell is wrong with you? Get over here!"

I desperately wanted to run away—away from that horrible smell and the vision of that dead cat dangling from the ceiling. But where would I go? I had no choice; I had to go back and hold that bag open.

I walked back over to Richard and took the bag. I held my breath to avoid the smell and shut my eyes tightly again to avoid seeing the dead cat. Richard dropped it into the bag, and the weight of it surprised me. "Do cats weigh more when they die?" I wondered.

"Seal the bag and take it out back behind the barn," Richard ordered.

"Then what?" I asked.

"Leave it," Richard said. He walked over to the kitchen sink and washed his hands. Then he went into the living room, as if throwing a dead cat into a feed bag was a normal, everyday occurrence.

I ran out of the house, holding the feed bag far in front of me. Instead of leaving it behind the barn as Richard had instructed, I took it to Indy's gravesite under the tree. There I dug another hole and buried that bag deep in the ground. Somehow, as I was digging the hole, my fear of the dead cat went away. All I felt for this helpless cat was sadness. I also felt as if I were doing something right by laying it to rest.

I patted the dirt down over the bag and then noticed something moving by my feet. It was the little tabby cat I had let loose in the cornfield, rubbing itself on my legs again. I picked it up and sobbed into its soft fur, apologizing for what Mom had done.

"Why, little kitty? Why did my mom do this? What did your friend do to make her so mad?" Of course I knew the cat wouldn't answer, but I had no one else to ask. This was one of the most horrible things I had ever witnessed, and what shocked me more than anything was that I was the only one upset about it.

"At least I can protect you," I said to the little tabby cat. I carried the cat through the long cornfield to the neighbors' farmhouse and knocked on the door. When old Mrs. Hopkins answered the door, she was clearly relieved to see the tabby cat.

"Felix!" Mrs. Hopkins exclaimed. "We've been looking everywhere for you! Now where is your brother?"

In that moment, I felt such guilt and shame that I couldn't even look Mrs. Hopkins in the eye as she took the cat in her arms.

"Sarah, thank you for bringing Felix home, sweetheart! Do you want Mr. Hopkins to give you a ride back?"

"No, but thank you! It's too nice out!" I said, forcing a smile onto my face.

"Well, if you see our other cat, Toby, will you send him on home, too?"

"Sure will!" I said, turning away. I couldn't stand there and lie anymore. It was too hard.

I made the long walk home and went back inside. Mom had dinner on the table. She and Richard and Emily were talking and laughing like they'd all just had the best days of their lives.

"Sit down, Sarah, you must be starving!" Mom greeted me.

"Mrs. Hopkins called to let us know that she appreciated you bringing her cat back," Richard said.

"Really?" I replied. "That was nice of her!"

"I dare her to let one of her stupid cats loose again!" Mom exclaimed. She and Richard laughed out loud as I sat there in shock.

From that day forward, I never went into the pantry again—and I always made sure to do a head count of the animals before and after school. I felt that I was their protector, and I promised that none of them would meet the same fate as that poor cat or my beloved goat, Indy. I also looked at Mom and Richard differently after that day. They had changed forever in my eyes. Now they were murderers.

= Chapter 5 =

Uncle Bill

Life on the farm didn't change much after the incidents with Indy and Toby. Mom was still abusive, Richard was at work most of the time, and Emily was the beloved daughter. I was twelve years old now, and my life consisted of going to school every day, coming home, doing my chores, and trying to avoid Mom at all costs.

One day I got off the school bus and was greeted at the door by a man I had never met before in my life.

"Hi! You must be Sarah!" he said.

I looked him up and down and immediately felt disgust in my stomach. The man looked like a complete bum: long, unwashed hair, unshaven face; dirty clothes; and sandals on his feet.

"Hi?" I said, with obvious confusion in my voice.

Mom came up behind him, and her face was glowing. She was well dressed, her hair was all done up, and her makeup was flawless. I couldn't remember the last time I had seen her look so good.

"Sarah, say hi to your uncle Bill!" Mom said.

"Oh!" I said. "Whose side of the family is he from?"

"He's not really your uncle, Sarah. Just a friend that you can call Uncle Bill."

Emily was standing behind me, unsure as to whether she should enter the house and come close to this unfamiliar man.

"Look what he brought you!" Mom exclaimed to me.

On the dining room table was a brand-new word processor. Immediately, I didn't care who this "Uncle Bill" was; I was taken aback by the beautiful piece of machinery on the table. Emily ran over to it, but Mom held her back. "No, sweetheart, that is for Sarah so she can do her schoolwork."

"Thank you!" I exclaimed to Bill.

"No problem—just want to make Nancy's girl's happy!" he replied.

"Can I use it before I start my chores?" I asked my mother.

"Of course. Take your time!"

I was in heaven. Not only was my mother being kind and sweet to me, but here was this awesome word processor sitting on the table, just waiting for me to start it up and type to my heart's content.

I sat down at the table, and Emily sat next to me. I turned the word processor on, and it hummed as if to say "Hello! What do you want to write about today?" I glanced up to say thank you again to "Uncle Bill" and noticed that he was getting ready to leave.

"See you later, Bill!" I said.

"See you around, Sarah!"

My mother was waiting at the kitchen door. Before Bill walked out the door, he stopped and leaned into Mom, as if he were going to kiss her on the mouth. Mom giggled like a schoolgirl and gently shoved him away "Tomorrow," she said quietly.

She shut the door behind him and turned around. Immediately, I could tell that the kind Mom was gone and the mother I knew was back. She crossed the kitchen in three large steps, leaned down, and got right into my face. "If you say one fucking word to your father about this, I will kill you . . . DO YOU UNDERSTAND ME?"

It became clear to me what was going on. This "Uncle Bill" was more than a friend; he was obviously close to Mom in a way that she and Richard were close.

"Get the hell out of here and do your chores." Mom picked up the word processor and hid it in a cabinet that Richard never looked in. "Did I stutter?" Mom asked. "Get off your fat ass and go do your chores!"

I got up slowly from the kitchen table and went to the front porch to put on my work boots. I was too young to fully understand what my mother was doing, but I wasn't completely naïve, either. Obviously, Mom was doing something she shouldn't be doing with this "Uncle Bill" or she wouldn't have snapped the way she did and hidden my present where Richard couldn't find it. But what could I do? I had been warned, and I didn't want to get beaten, so I knew I would just keep my mouth shut.

Later that evening, the whole family was sitting at the dinner table eating a delicious meal of pork chops, corn on the cob, and salad. Mom kept glaring across the table at me between bites. Then a strange, whirring sound came from the cabinet in which Mom had hidden the word processor.

"What the hell is that noise, Nancy?" Richard asked.

To my surprise, Emily piped up and said, "That's Sarah's present from Uncle Bill!"

"Who the fuck is Uncle Bill?" Richard demanded, slamming his fork down and getting up to see my present for himself.

I looked up and had to fight to keep a grin from forming on my face. Finally, Mom was going to get caught. She was going to be in trouble, and Richard was going to yell at her for a change. I sat back in my chair and waited to see what Mom would do.

Mom didn't miss a beat. "Oh, you know, Bill, the delivery man from FS Oil. He dropped that off today with the oil delivery because his daughter didn't use it anymore. I thought Sarah might get some use out of it!"

"Oh, come on!" I thought to myself. Uncle Bill wasn't an oil delivery guy; he had left the farmhouse earlier that day in a ratty old blue pickup truck.

Richard opened the cabinet and took out the word processor. "This is an awfully nice thing to be giving away, don't you think?" he asked Mom.

"I know, I couldn't believe it either!" she exclaimed in a high-pitched voice.

Mom shot me another dirty look over the table. "Did you see that Sarah gave the horses bad hay? Buddy has had a cough for two days now. I'm going to have to call the vet."

I looked at my mother in shock. How in the world did this go from Mom getting presents from some weird guy to a complete lie about Buddy being sick?

Richard immediately turned on me. "You think money grows on trees, bitch? Do you have the money to pay the vet because you were too damn lazy to notice that you were giving the horses moldy hay?"

"Dad, I didn't give the horses moldy hay! I haven't noticed Buddy coughing."

"Are you calling me a liar?" Mom screamed over the table at me.

SMACK! Richard had come up behind me and whacked me in the back of the head with such force that I smacked my face against the top of the kitchen table. Emily started crying, and Mom quickly ushered her out of the room. Richard pulled my short hair and yanked my head back. "Lie to me, will you? Nancy, it's time for Sarah to write tonight!"

Writing as punishment meant staying up until the wee hours of the morning—sometimes in my room, sometimes at a tray table in the bathroom—with a pencil and a piece of paper, writing *I will not lie* over and over and over until Mom was satisfied.

Tears streamed down my face, and I wiped my nose. Then I noticed that my hand was covered in blood.

"Jesus Christ . . . NANCY!" Richard bellowed. Mom came storming into the kitchen.

"Clean her up, will you?" Richard left the room, and Mom threw a stack of napkins at me.

"Wipe your fucking nose," Mom said, "and you'd better get started on your chores because you have a lot of writing to do."

I rushed outside, stuffing napkins up my nose to stop the bleeding. I ran down to the horse barn and sat in the corner, sobbing and screaming into my hand. "Buddy isn't sick! I didn't give him bad hay!" I kept saying over and over.

Buddy came into the stall where I was sitting and crying. He looked at me with his big brown eyes. I pleaded, "You aren't sick, are you, Buddy? I didn't make you sick, did I?" Buddy just stood there, looking at me. I stood up and threw my arms around his neck and hugged him as tightly as I could. Buddy stood motionless, as if he knew that I needed love at that moment.

I finally got my nose to stop bleeding and walked up to the barn where the hay was kept. I turned on the light and closely inspected the hay bales. "There's no moldy hay in here," I said angrily to myself. Nevertheless, no one was going to believe me, and I had to finish my chores. I had a lot of writing to do. I spent the next five hours writing *I will not lie* over and over and over until I couldn't hold the pencil anymore.

After that, Mom introduced me to many more "uncles." She knew that after that horrible night I would never mention a word to Richard about any men who came around while he was at work. Emily was spared the physical abuse or any other repercussions that I received that night and was never again exposed to any of Mom's boyfriends. I, on the other hand, met many men in the next year. They ranged from oil delivery workers to construction workers to car dealership workers. I would accompany my mother on her "dates" so Richard would not become suspicious. I usually ended up sitting in the car or in another room while Mom was having fun with her boy toy of the moment.

By the time I turned thirteen, I had met nine different "uncles," all of whom showered me with gifts. Each one was only around for about a month. But I didn't dare speak a word about them to Richard, for I knew that would only lead to another beating and another long night of sitting in the bathroom writing sentences. I was focused on survival, on protecting myself from harm—and if I were to utter a word about my mother's indiscretions to Richard, I would be putting my life in danger.

Chapter 6

The five-finger discount

Life was getting tougher on the farm. Mom and Richard were constantly stressed about money, and they took their anger out on me on a nightly basis. Some nights it was just verbal abuse and name-calling, but many nights it was punches and kicks.

Sometimes I wondered if anyone knew what was going on. I couldn't figure out how I could go to school with bruises all over my body and cuts on my face without one person asking me what was going on. Like I would have told the truth anyway!

Once in a while, a nice lady from the Department of Children and Family Services (DCFS) would show up because of an anonymous tip and ask me questions about the bruises on my body, but I always lied. I knew that if I didn't live at home, I would end up in foster care, and I did NOT want that for my life. So I would tell the DCFS lady my grand stories of falling down the stairs or getting kicked by a horse; then she would leave and I wouldn't hear from her again.

Of course, after every DCFS visit, Mom would beat me worse than ever. "Who the fuck are you to call the authorities on me? I'll kill you, you worthless piece of shit!" Mom's fists would rain down on me, her boots slamming into my side, and she would pull my hair practically out of my head. No matter how many times I told her that I hadn't called DCFS, it didn't matter. It was an excuse for Mom to beat me.

"What can I do to make her love me?" I would think to myself as I lay in bed, shaking and trembling from my most recent beating. The answer eventually came in the form of what is sometimes called the "five-finger discount."

It all began on a family trip to an outlet mall. Mom, Richard, Emily, and I were walking around a store that sold everything from videos to snowshoes. I wandered away from the rest of the family to check out the new Keds shoes that were on display. I desperately wanted a pair of those shoes. Every girl in school had a pair, and I thought that if I had a pair, I just might fit in with these girls who teased me every day.

Mom walked over and said, "Forget it! There's no way you are getting shoes that cost that much." Her voice cut off. "Unless . . ."

"Unless what?" I asked, a glimmer of hope in my voice.

"Do you have your purse?"

In reply, I held up the enormous purse my mother had bought me earlier that week. It was brown, cheap fake leather, and obscenely oversized, but it was my first purse and I loved it.

"Come with me," Mom said. She pulled a pair of Keds off the rack, double-checked the size, and then pulled me to a back corner of the store. "Open your purse," she said. I opened my purse, and Mom shoved the shoes into it. "Now put these in there, too, and don't act stupid." Mom shoved two movies into my oversized purse and zipped it up.

My stomach knotted. I had just turned into a shoplifter, and my mother had taught me how to do it! Not quite knowing how to react, I tried to act nonchalant as I walked out of the store, holding my breath. I was just waiting for a store clerk to run out and grab me and take me to prison. But nothing happened. I left the store with a new pair of shoes and two new movies and nothing happened!

Mom came up to me and gave me a hug, one of the few times in my life I could remember her touching me with love. "I'm so proud of you," she said. "Wasn't that fun?"

I nodded, overcome with mixed emotions. I knew that I had just committed a crime, but my mother was so proud of me that I overlooked the criminal aspect and just basked in this rare moment of love from Mom.

From then on, Mom was unstoppable. Every day was a new shopping trip, a new thing to steal. Some days Mom was shoving roasts into my purse, other days it was perfume or new clothes. She taught me how to check for security tags on movies and how to remove the security tags from clothes so we could get them out of department stores. I did as I was told. If Mom wanted me to steal something, I stole it. If I didn't steal something quickly enough or I argued about it, Mom would grab me in the store, digging her fingernails into my arm, and whisper into my ear, "You either take that now, you little bitch, or I'll call the manager over here and have you arrested for the things you already have in your purse."

Mom always justified the shoplifting by stating how little money we had and saying that we needed these things to survive. I understood that to an extent, but Mom had me stealing so much that I soon grew tired of going to stores with her, hiding in corners, checking for security tags, and looking up at the ceiling for cameras. I thought that Richard would be upset about our shoplifting, but he participated at times, shoving things into my purse or my winter jacket right along with Mom. All I knew for sure was that after an especially good shoplifting experience, Mom would treat me like gold, and there would be a day of no beatings and no name-calling. So I stole what Mom told me to steal and prayed that no one saw or found out.

One day, however, I decided that enough was enough. It was getting close to Christmas, and again the family was short on cash. Buddy had slipped on the ice and cut his leg open. Mom and Richard said they couldn't afford both the vet bill and Christmas presents. This meant it was time to go to the mall and shoplift.

The whole family got into our big Suburban and headed toward the highway that led to the mall, which was forty-five minutes away. I was tired of these shoplifting trips, but what choice did I have? I leaned my head on the window and looked up at the sky, wishing my parents were rich enough to afford what we needed without the hassle of stuffing clothes and other things into my purse.

Richard suddenly pulled over to the side of the road and pointed to a small cemetery that looked as though it had been around since the beginning of time. "Look at those decorations on that headstone, Nancy. You could make something like that!" I strained to see what Richard was talking about, but all I could see were rows of headstones.

"Make something like that? Pull in there, Richard!"

I had no idea what was going on. We had no family in this cemetery, no friends buried here. There was no reason for us to be pulling into the cemetery at all. But I kept quiet in the backseat as Richard maneuvered the large Suburban along the tiny roads in the cemetery and came to a stop in front of a small headstone, adorned with a beautiful Christmas wreath.

Emily piped up from her seat: "Mommy, where are we?"

"Don't worry about it, Emily, just sit back and read your book."

Emily was more than happy to oblige. I watched in horror as my mother jumped out of the passenger door and ran up to the headstone. Mom stood in front of the headstone, took a good look around, and then snatched up the wreath and dashed back into the Suburban.

Richard laughed. "That's too pretty for a dead person to enjoy!" he said with a smile on his face.

Mom laughed along with him. "Won't this look pretty on our front door?"

I sat in stunned silence. I had just witnessed my mother stealing flowers from someone's grave. I couldn't comprehend it. Why would my mother do this? Why not just have me steal a wreath from a store instead of taking from people who couldn't even defend themselves?

"Drive around some more, Richard. Let's see what else there is."

I couldn't keep quiet any longer. "Stop it, Mom! You can't steal things from dead people."

Mom acted like she didn't hear me, or maybe she really didn't hear me. She was absolutely consumed with surveying the rest of the graveyard, eyeing the winter hanging baskets and winter flowers that adorned the graves. Soon, another wreath caught her eye.

"Stop, Richard!" Mom ordered. "Sarah, get out and get that wreath with the red balls on it."

I looked out my window at the headstone. It was a child's grave. I knew this because the child's face was carved into the headstone. My heart broke. I couldn't do it, and I knew that I had to stand up to Mom on this one.

"No, Mom, I won't do it," I said rather meekly.

Before I could get all the words out of my mouth, Mom had jumped over her seat and into the 2nd seat of the surburban. . She slapped me across the face so hard it made my ears ring. "What do you mean, no? NO? Get out and get that wreath before we get caught! Do you want me to go to jail?"

It took every ounce of my energy not to say, "Actually, yes, I would love for you to spend the rest of your life in a rat-infested prison, right where you belong!" Instead, although I knew it would mean a harder beating, I said, "NO, Mom! I am not doing it!" I couldn't comply with this order. Stealing roasts and clothes for Mom was one thing; stealing flowers from a child's grave was another.

Mom grabbed me by the hair and yanked me over the seat (the surburban had 3 rows of seats). I screamed in pain and covered my face, not knowing what was coming next. As Mom dragged me over the backseat, my arm accidentally hit Emily in the side of the head. Emily cried out and Richard turned around, rage flaming in his eyes.

"Get that bitch out of the vehicle now!" he screamed.

"With pleasure," Mom said.

I was still screaming in pain from the hair-pulling when I felt my legs being pulled out of the Suburban. Richard had gotten out and was yanking me out of the vehicle with such force that I thought my legs were going to break.

"Leave her fat ass here!" Mom shouted. Richard threw me onto the ground and got back into the Suburban.

"No, please don't leave me here!" I screamed.

My screaming was to no avail. Richard slammed his foot down on the accelerator and took off out of the cemetery with Mom and Emily. I was left there in the cold next to this child's grave, watching as my family drove away. I had no idea where I was or how far away I was from the farmhouse. So I sat and waited and cried. For the first time, I wished I were dead like the child whose grave I was sitting by.

"Maybe if I were dead," I thought, "they would love me." This was the first time in all the years of beating and ridiculing that I had ever wanted to give up on living.

It may have been forty-five minutes or it may have been two hours before I saw the Suburban pull back into the cemetery. I was numb from the tops of my ears to the tips of my toes. No one said a word to me as I crawled into the backseat and curled into a ball to warm up. As a matter of fact, no one said a word to me for the rest of the day. We drove back to the farmhouse, and I got out of the Surburban and headed down to the barn to feed the horses.

Suicidal thoughts were racing through my head. I kept thinking about my family leaving me alone, in the cold, in a graveyard as punishment for not stealing a Christmas wreath from a child's headstone. Then I thought about that child, wondered how he had died, and eventually smiled to myself. "I won!" I realized. "They didn't get to steal that wreath. I WON!"

The suicidal thoughts left my head as I realized that although I was numb, hungry, sore, and cold, I had fought for a child who couldn't fight for himself. I had done the right thing and stood up to my tyrannical parents.

"Maybe it will be a Merry Christmas this year after all!" I thought.

Chapter 7

Melissa sees . . .

It was a beautiful spring day at the farmhouse. The birds were singing and the sweet smell of hay wafted through the air. I was saddling up one of the horses to go for a ride when Emily came running up, her long hair streaming behind her and her eyes wild.

"Sarah!" Emily cried out. "We're moving again!"

Joy surged through my veins. Finally, we were going to get off that farm? It was too good to be true. "Do you know where?" I asked Emily excitedly.

"I-t-t-t's-s-s a h-h-house across from Daddy's work," she stuttered. Emily had developed a stuttering problem, rather severe at times. She had also started sleepwalking almost every night. Mom claimed that Emily stuttered because of playing Nintendo games, but I knew that Emily stuttered because of the violence and craziness she witnessed on a daily basis. My heart had softened toward Emily, knowing that she was dealing with my abuse in her own way. In a way, I felt responsible for her stuttering problem.

I smiled at Emily and took the saddle off the mare. "We'll have to do this later, Daisy Mae!" I said. I put Daisy back into the pasture and followed Emily into the farmhouse.

Mom was on the phone with one of her boyfriends. "Walnut, Illinois—some little town out in the middle of nowhere, but right across the street from Richard's work. Well, of course I'll try to see you . . ." Mom turned and noticed us standing there. She angrily waved us out of the room so she could have her privacy.

"Walnut?" I thought. I had never heard of that town before, but if it had people within walking distance, I was going to be happy!

I was now fourteen, hitting puberty, becoming interested in boys, and dying for companionship beyond the farm animals. Mom had let my hair grow out some. I had gotten taller and leaner, and the rest of my body was starting to take the form of a woman. But it seemed that the taller and more shapely I got, the more violent my mother became.

Mom had moved on from calling me "loser" and "bitch" to making up nicknames that tortured me mentally. Mom would now kick me in the kidney area during beatings and scream "Kidney Kate!" in reference to kidney problems I'd had when I was younger. As my lips got fuller and my face filled out, she would pull on my lips and scream "Nigger Lips!" As my legs and rear end changed, "Thunder Thighs!" and "Bubble Butt!" would be yelled in my face.

Emily wasn't immune to the name-calling, either. When Emily stuttered and embarrassed Mom in public, Mom would mock Emily all the way home, imitating her stuttering and calling her "Stuttering Sue." This broke my heart. More than once, I took a beating for standing up to Mom when she was mocking Emily at the dinner table.

Knowing that we would be moving to an actual town, with actual neighbors, made my heart sing. Neighbors meant that Mom would have to cut back on the beatings. Neighbors meant possible girlfriends and a maybe even a new "Debbie." I wouldn't be so desperately lonely anymore. This couldn't be better news!

Just as before, we were packed up and ready to move in less than a week. We had to sell all the farm animals, and that week during my chores I said good-bye to them all and spent some extra time with them. Each of those animals held a special place in my heart. They had helped me through my toughest times on the farm. I knew I would miss them very much and never forget them. I put fresh spring flowers on Indy's and the cat's graves behind the barn and said my good-byes to them also.

Finally, after five days of nonstop packing, we were ready to go. Richard backed out of the driveway and I took one more look out of the Surburban window. I would never forget this farmhouse—never forget the horrors and torture I had endured there. But I was still alive! I had made it, and now I could begin the next chapter in my life.

During the forty-five minute drive to Walnut, there was very little talking going on. Mom was sulking, Richard just drove and listened to the radio, and Emily and I sat and stared out the window.

As we got closer to Walnut, my heart began to race. I could see a little park, the water tower, businesses, and lots of little houses. It looked like heaven, and I couldn't wait to get to our new home.

Richard made a couple of turns down some side streets and came to a stop in front of our new home. It was a little white house, with a garage on the corner. There was a flower garden in the front and a little deck out to the side. I could already see kids my age playing and hanging out in their front yards, looking and pointing at the new neighbors that had just pulled up.

"Home sweet home!" Richard said cheerfully.

I jumped out and took a deep breath. "It smells like sausage and cheese!" I said.

"There is a cheese factory right down the street," Richard said as he opened up the back of the U-Haul.

"Could this be any more perfect?" I wondered.

Mom finally dragged herself out of the front seat and stood in the front yard. She took a good look around. "Well, isn't this just great," she said loudly. She gave Richard a dirty look and grabbed the house keys from him. Emily and I could barely contain our excitement as Mom opened the door to our new home.

It was an extremely small house, but to me it was just perfect. Emily and I had our own rooms, and there was a cute little kitchen with a window that looked out into the backyard. Out the front door was a park and Richard's work right across the street.

"Where is the school?" I asked my mother.

"I have no fucking idea, Sarah. Ask the son-of-a-bitch who moved us here."

No matter how hard my mother was trying to bring the mood down, it wasn't going to work. Richard, Emily, and I spent the rest of the afternoon unloading the U-Haul and getting everything into the house and the garage. Later that evening, Richard took Emily and me for a drive around town. Everything was so quaint and cute. The school looked like something right out of a storybook, and I couldn't wait to start there and make friends.

I wasn't waiting long. Two days after we moved in, I started school. I was so nervous on my first day, worried about being judged, worried about finding friends and hopefully a boyfriend. I stood in front of the mirror that morning and heard

Sarah Burleton

my mother's taunts in my head... "Thunder Thighs!" "Kidney Kate!" All the good feelings I had about myself vanished as I nervously rubbed my pant legs and tried to see if my butt really stuck out as far as my mother said it did.

"What the hell are you doing, Sarah?" Mom had been standing at my door, watching me look at myself in the mirror.

"Nothing," I said.

"Making yourself look like a whore, are you?"

"No, Mom!"

"How much hair spray do you have in your hair?" Mom walked over and grabbed my bangs and pulled. "Look at this shit in your hair; go wash it out!"

"Mom, I don't have time. I have to get to school."

I picked up my bag and tried to get out of my bedroom door, but Mom was standing in the way with her arms out. "Wash your hair or I'll wash it for you," she said calmly.

I refused, repeating, "Mom, I don't have time!" I really didn't. I had to go to school early to meet my homeroom teacher for a tour of the school.

Mom dropped her arms, looked me up and down, and laughed out loud. "I guess if you think that looks good, more power to you!"

I put my head down, and tears welled up in my eyes. "Not this morning!" I said to myself.

"Your shoes are down in the basement," Mom said with a smile on her face. I pushed past her and went to the landing. Mom came up behind me, and WHAM! She kicked me in the back, and I went flying down the stairs. I landed on the bottom step, directly on my tailbone. I felt my breath stop, and I turned my head and looked back up at Mom with tears streaming down my face. "It... hurts," I stammered, barely able to speak.

"Oh, get up, you fucking retard!" Mom said. She picked up my book bag and threw it down the stairs at me. "You'd better hurry, or you're going to be late," she said before she turned away and busied herself in the kitchen.

I managed to stand up and slip my shoes on. "Great first day!" I thought to myself. I made it back up the stairs with my bag and walked out the back door.

It took me over forty-five minutes to walk the three blocks to school that morning because of the excruciating pain in my tailbone. I was a nervous wreck walking into the school for the first time. Not only was I late for my school tour, but also I was afraid that the other kids would make fun of the way I was walking.

I took a deep breath and entered the building. Immediately, I was greeted by a girl my age—a girl who would soon be my new best friend. "Hi, I'm Melissa," she said cheerfully. "You must be Sarah!"

From that day forward, Melissa and I were inseparable. We played basketball together, were both in track, spent the night at each other's houses, and even went to an NBA game together. However, I never felt that I could be truly honest with Melissa about my mother. For some odd reason, Mom and Melissa got along extremely well, so I didn't think Melissa would believe me or be my friend anymore if I told her the truth about what went on behind our closed doors.

Like every other good thing in my life, my friendship with Melissa would ultimately be taken from me. Although our family had moved away from the farmhouse and we were a bit better off financially, Mom's old habits eventually resurfaced. She found a new mall to shoplift from, and once again she made me go every weekend for a new shoplifting adventure. If I refused, I received the same beatings as before—Mom just didn't yell so loudly. If I showed any hesitance to shoplift in the stores, Mom would start berating me and making fun of the way I looked in front of other customers: "God, you really squeezed into those jeans, didn't you? Look at those cow hocks! Look how stupid your hair looks today!"

I would keep my head down and glance up occasionally to see the customers' reactions to my mother's taunts. Mostly, people would just stare, but once in a while I would catch someone laughing at the things my mother said to me. "They must think my mom is right," I would think to myself. Slowly, my mother's taunts began to affect the way I saw myself in the mirror. Gone was the tall, shapely girl from the farm; all that looked back at me in the mirror was a fat, ugly girl whom no one wanted.

One day after school, right out of the blue, Mom looked at me and asked, "Do you want Melissa to come over and spend the night?"

I looked up at her in surprise and wondered what kind of trick this was. "Sure," I said hesitantly.

"We'll drive to Princeton and have dinner—how does that sound?"

Nothing seemed out of the ordinary, so I jumped up and called Melissa right away. "Yay!" Melissa said when I invited her to come. "I'll see you in twenty minutes!"

As promised, twenty minutes later Melissa was at the door with her backpack. I let her in, and she ran and gave my mom a huge hug. I watched them and got very sad for a moment, wondering why I couldn't count five times my mother had given me a hug like that.

"Ready to go to Princeton?" Mom asked Melissa.

"Oh, yeah—Monical's, here we come!"

Mom, Melissa, and I piled into the Surburban and headed toward Princeton. Melissa sat in the front seat with Mom, and for the next half hour they chatted about everything from cooking to sewing. I listened and tried to contribute to the conversation, but Mom would cut me off and tell me not to interrupt.

"Yeah, Sarah, don't interrupt!" Melissa would say, laughing along with Mom.

As we drove into town, Mom said, "Let's make a pit stop before dinner." I looked out the window and saw that we were pulling into the mall parking lot. My heart sank.

"Oh, God—don't steal in front of Melissa," I thought. Then I said to Mom, "I don't feel like going in."

"Melissa, would you give us a second?" Mom asked.

"Sure!"

Melissa jumped out of the front seat and got busy fixing her makeup outside as Mom turned around and looked at me. She grabbed my arm and dug in her fingernails. "You still have to go home with me, little girl," she said in a low tone.

I had no choice; I had to get out and follow Melissa and my mother into the mall. Once inside, they hightailed it toward the craft store, and Mom led Melissa back to the yarn section. Within seconds, Mom was stuffing rolls of yarn into her purse and motioning for me to come over. Melissa was standing there with a look of complete shock on her face. I didn't want to go over there; I knew that Mom would make me stuff merchandise into my purse, too, and I didn't want Melissa to see that. But I also knew the consequences if I did not shoplift, and my fear of my mother outweighed my sense of right and wrong and and my desire to do the right thing in front of Melissa.

As I stuffed rolls of yarn into my purse next to my mother, I could feel Melissa's eyes boring into my back. I couldn't even look at her as I turned and zipped up my purse. Melissa stood motionless as Mom and I headed to the store entrance. "Come on, Melissa, let's go," Mom said.

Melissa shot a look at me and a look around the store. For a moment, I thought she was going to tell on me and have me arrested. But, to my surprise, Melissa smiled at Mom and followed her out of the store.

There was no talking on the way back to the truck. As Mom pulled out of the mall parking lot, Melissa said quietly, "I'm not feeling well. I think I need to go home."

"Are you sure?" Mom asked, feigning concern.

"Yeah. I think it's the heat, or something I ate."

I didn't say a word. I knew why Melissa was going home, and I didn't blame her a bit.

There was no chatter between Mom and Melissa on the way home, and when Mom pulled into Melissa's driveway, Melissa jumped out and ran into her house without saying a word.

"Think you'll be seeing her again?" Mom asked me.

I didn't reply. Of course I wouldn't be seeing Melissa again. Melissa had morals. She was a good girl who had a good mom; she wouldn't want to be friends with me anymore. I went to bed that night dreading school the next day, knowing that everyone would have heard what we did in the craft store.

I wasn't wrong. The next day, a group of kids from my class—including Melissa—was outside the school waiting for me. When I arrived, they began taunting me, calling me names like "Thief" and "Harvester." They spent the day chanting these names at me in the school hallways. They stuck Post-it notes with my new names scrawled on them onto my back. The perfect town with the perfect school and the perfect friends had turned into a dark nightmare for me. Now, once again, I had no escape, no one to run to. I was all alone again.

I made it through the school day and then walked home. My stomach was in knots. The names I had been called all day were running through my head along with the names my mother called me. I felt like running headlong into the train that was passing by, ending my life at that moment just to finally have peace. I started agreeing with my mother and the kids at school: "I am a thief! I did steal! I am fat and gross! Look at me, I have the biggest ass in school!"

As I reached the front steps of my house, I doubled over in pain and threw up on the sidewalk. Mom came running out. "Oh, God, you're disgusting," she said. "Get inside and stay in your room! I don't want you getting any of us sick."

I was more than happy to oblige. All I wanted to do was go to bed anyway, to avoid any more name-calling. I went to my room and took off my clothes and looked in the mirror. "You fat pig! You worthless piece of shit!" I started saying to my reflection. "You deserve nothing—cow!"

I felt my life was over. I was trapped again—but this time, instead of just being treated like dirt at home, I was going to get it at school, too. I spit at my reflection, collapsed on my bed, and sobbed until I was spent. My stomach growled in hunger, and I found myself enjoying the pain. It gave me something else to think about.

= Chapter 8 =

Anorexic Annie

Not long after the Melissa debacle, I started to become depressed. I found it hard to eat; I was physically tired of being beaten all the time; and I had nowhere to run where anyone would treat me with kindness. I was fourteen years old and had no control over my life whatsoever. My mood depended on how my mother was feeling. But even if I left for school in the morning in a good mood, I would still be treated like scum by my peers.

Since the shoplifting incident, the kids at school had completely turned on me. They had no trouble finding reasons to pick on me, and they would relentlessly tease me about things for weeks at a time. I had no friends, no boys interested in me, and I felt completely alone. I started to punish myself mentally: I would look in the mirror and see a fat, ugly, worthless human being staring back at me. I felt lost and unloved, and I needed an answer to my problems.

One winter morning, I woke up feeling quite cranky. I had not eaten well the day before and had had a tough time getting to sleep. My stomach hurt and my head ached, but I didn't dare complain. The last thing I wanted was to stay home from school with Mom.

I walked upstairs and passed Mom in the kitchen.

"Morning, Mom," I said.

"Mmm-hmm." Mom looked up at me. "Jesus—you look like shit." She looked at Emily, who was sitting at the table, and said, "How's my pretty little girl doing?"

I put my head down and walked out of the room. I went into the bathroom, shut the door, stripped off all my clothes, and stood on the scale.

"I lost five pounds?" I said to myself. I got off the scale, checked it, and stood on it again. "140 pounds?" I was 145 just two days ago! How did I lose five pounds so fast? My stomach growled, and my eyes lit up.

"I didn't eat!" I thought excitedly. "I am finally losing weight!"

Maybe now Mom wouldn't call me names and make fun of my thunder thighs or cow hocks. Maybe now the boys would like me and the girls would invite me to their sleep-overs again. It was almost too much for me to handle! I had barely had time to bask in the warmth of the new love I thought I would get when my mother yelled, "I don't hear that shower running!"

For the rest of the morning I was in a daze. Mom had made eggs and bacon for breakfast, but I didn't eat. I made up an excuse about my stomach hurting and said I would eat when I got to school. Surprisingly, Mom bought my story and didn't give me any grief about it before I left for school. As I headed toward the front door, I spied Mom's lip gloss on the floor and snatched it up. "I want to feel pretty today," I said to myself. As I walked to school, I applied Mom's lip gloss over and over and imagined myself as one of those pretty girls at school or one of the thin, beautiful actresses on television.

I spent the rest of the day thinking about losing weight. It was the first day since the shoplifting incident that I walked through the hallways with my head held high and I was able to tune out the jabs and jeers from the other kids. I refrained from eating lunch or any snacks during the day and could swear that I felt the weight just slipping off my body. I couldn't wait to get home and stand on the scale again and see if anything had changed.

Once the final bell had rung, I bolted out of school and ran home. Mom wasn't home, so I let myself in, ran to the bathroom, stripped off my clothes, and stood on the scale. A wave of disappointment crashed over me. "Still 140 pounds?" I thought. "I have to eat less."

My mood had gone from great to bad in a matter of seconds. I was pacing in my room, trying to figure out a way to lose more weight, when I heard my mother come in the front door.

"Sarah! Come up and help me with these groceries!"

"Oh, God! It's almost dinnertime! I can't eat!" I thought in a panic.

I rushed upstairs and started unloading the grocery bags stacked on the kitchen table. "OK, salad, I can eat that. . . . Little Debbie cakes . . . how many calories do these have? . . . Oh, no way am I eating that!" My mind was racing as I considered what I could and couldn't eat.

"What's for dinner tonight?" I asked Mom.

"Homemade pizza," Mom replied.

"Crap!" I thought. "Well, I can scrape the topping off and just eat the crust. . . ."

Thinking about the pizza was consuming me. I couldn't hear anything around me as I thought about how I was going to get out of eating that pizza.

SMACK! My head stung and my eyes watered. I blinked and ducked, instinctively covering my face.

"Take your hands off your face!" Mom screamed. "Show me your pretty face!"

I had no idea what had caused this, no idea what I had done to make my mother scream.

"Lip gloss! Lip gloss! WHORE! You don't need to wear that shit!" Mom was screaming so loudly now that spit was flying out of her mouth and hitting my hands, which were still covering my face.

"Lip gloss?" I thought. Then it hit me: I had forgotten to take Mom's lip gloss out of my pocket—the lip gloss I had spent the morning applying because it made me feel pretty. .

"Wait a minute—this is MY lip gloss?" Mom screamed into my face .

I peered through my fingers at my mother. I had never seen Mom's face change like that before. It was as if she became someone else in a matter of seconds. Her eyes shifted and narrowed, her mouth became a sneer, and her jaw clenched.

Mom's hands clamped around my throat. My hands came away from my face as I struggled to free myself from her grasp.

"M-m-m-m-om!" I heard Emily stuttering from the corner, but Mom paid no attention. Her fingernails dug in tighter around my neck.

I couldn't breathe; my eyes started to bug; and my heart began to race. I fought harder against Mom, trying to pry her fingernails out of my neck. Then, for some reason, Mom let go. I collapsed onto the couch, sputtering and crying, gulping fresh air into my lungs.

"Look at me!" Mom ordered. Terrified, I turned toward her. But before I could look my mother in the eyes, a force unlike anything I had felt before in my life smashed into my jaw. My eyes rolled, my entire jaw seemed to shift to the opposite side of my face, and my cheekbone felt like it was crushed.

I leaned my head back against the couch and forced my eyes onto my mother. She was standing above me with a large glass paperweight in her hands.

"Don't you shut your eyes!" Mom said in a panic. "EMILY! Get some water!"

I started to shut my eyes, my head spinning and my jaw throbbing. I wanted to shut my eyes and never wake up, but Mom wasn't letting me do that.

"Sit up and drink this," she said almost lovingly.

I forced my eyes open and sat up. I took a small sip of the water and whispered, "Can I go downstairs and lie down?"

Mom got down on her knees and looked at my face. "Look at me!" she ordered. She held up her finger and moved it as she said, "Look up, look down, look left, look right."

I complied, following my mother's finger with my eyes. It was painful to move my eyes, but I was able to follow my mother's orders.

"Go on; go lie down," she said.

Shakily, I got to my feet and made it downstairs to my room in the basement. I collapsed on the bed and put my sore face into my pillow. It wasn't long before the pillow was sopping wet from my tears. "I knew better!" I said to myself. "That goddamn lip gloss!" I could have kicked myself. Had I just remembered to take it out of my pocket when I got home, I wouldn't be in this situation.

My stomach growled. That was a good pain. My tears stopped flowing as I felt my stomach rumble, and it occurred to me that I wouldn't have to eat dinner that night. Suddenly, my face didn't hurt as much and I didn't feel as bad. I thought of losing five or ten more pounds and how good that would make me feel and look. I had found a way to put a smile on my face before I went to sleep for the rest of the evening.

After that, I began starving myself on a daily basis. The numbers on the scale continued to go down. The stomach pains helped make the pain from Mom's beatings go away. As I got skinnier, I started receiving compliments from the kids at school; this made me even more determined to lose as much weight as I could.

Soon none of my clothes were fitting, my ribs were show-ing, and my face was becoming gaunt. People at school stopped making fun of me for stealing and started whispering about my new appearance behind my back. The compliments stopped coming, and people looked at me with concern in their eyes. Mom stopped making Thunder Thigh remarks and started to tease me about other body parts, such as my "Bug Eyes," my "Nigger Lips," and my "Ape Feet." When Mom teased me, I restricted my food intake even more to make myself feel better. My life was absolutely consumed by the numbers on the scale and the food that entered my mouth. It was becoming apparent to all those around me that there was a problem.

One day at school I was called into the nurse's office. Sit-ting in there were my mom, Richard, the nurse, and the prin-cipal. The principal stood up and said, "Hi, Sarah, do you mind sitting down for a minute?"

The nurse came over and put a blood pressure cuff on my arm. I observed as she worked the pump and watched her wristwatch, wondering what the problem was. The nurse looked up at Mom and Richard and shook her head.

"It's low, it's real low," she said. She looked sadly at me and stroked the side of my face. "What are you doing to yourself, sweetheart?" she asked.

"Yes, Sarah, what ARE you doing to yourself?" my mother asked with a tone of sarcasm in her voice.

"Now, Mrs. Burleton , let's stay calm. This is about Sarah now," the principal said as he sat back down in his chair.

Suddenly the nurse's office closed in on me, and my throat grew tight. "They found out!" I thought in horror.

"Sarah, are you starving yourself?" the principal asked with a quaver in his voice.

I summoned my courage and looked up. "Yes," I said softly.

Richard put his head in his hands, and Mom sat back in her chair and crossed her arms.

"Do you want to talk about it?" the principal asked in a soft tone.

"No!" I said, rather defiantly.

"Could you sit in the hall for a minute?" the principal asked.

Without a word, I got up and stormed out of the office. I was furious: furious that someone had learned my secret, furious that Mom had found out, furious that they were going to take away the only thing I had control of in my life. "Run away, Sarah!" my mind kept telling me. But before I could get up, the nurse came out into the hallway.

"Let's go to your locker and get your books," she said in a kind voice.

"What's going on?" I asked.

"I'll let your parents tell you. Don't worry about it, Sarah. Everything is going to be OK now."

I got my books and followed the nurse outside, where Mom, Richard, and the principal were waiting for me. "Good luck, Sarah," the principal said as he gave me a hug. Richard put his arm around my shoulders and led me toward the car.

Once we were inside the car and safely away from the school, Mom turned around and looked at me with fire in her eyes. "Now I have to send you to a clinic because you won't eat?" she screamed. I started crying. "SHUT UP, you fucking mistake! What a BIG mistake you were, Anorexic Annie!"

I stopped crying and sat there in disbelief. I was anorexic? That's what I was? Now I was diseased, had a clinical disorder? I'd thought I was just skinny, not anorexic. Now I was going to a clinic for help? "What kind of clinic?" I asked.

"A clinic for stupid kids," Richard said.

"A clinic for crazies so they can attempt to be normal again," added Mom.

The rest of the day was a blur. Richard and Mom packed a bag for me and had me admitted into an in-patient treatment center before nightfall. I spent the evening feeling like a caged dog. There were doctors in white coats walking around, and crazy kids strapped to their beds being wheeled in. Someone was watching me while I went to the bathroom, watching me while I ate, even watching me while I slept, making sure that I didn't make myself sick or get rid of the food that I had been forced to eat for dinner.

I had lost complete control. In a matter of a few hours, I had gone from doing OK at home and school to being committed to a treatment center where right down the hall was a child in a straightjacket, screaming obscenities at the top of his lungs. "I've got to figure out a way to get out of here!" I thought in panic.

For the next two weeks, I focused on getting out. I told the psychiatrists what they wanted to hear; I made up stories about why I'd started to starve myself; I ate with a smile on my face and managed to keep the food down. Not once did I talk about the mental and physical abuse I suffered at the hands of my mother. That would have just meant more time in the psychiatrist's office and more time in that damn clinic. And lo and behold, after two weeks I got my discharge papers!

Richard and Mom came to pick me up after my two-week stay. At the clinic, they hovered all over me, hugging me and helping me put my bags into the car. After we pulled away and I had waved to the last nurse out the window, Mom turned around and said, "Well, Anorexic Annie, they sure fattened you up again, didn't they?"

"Why does it have to be me?" I thought as tears streamed down my face. "Why me?"

= Chapter 9 =

Homecoming

I didn't change much after my trip to the in-patient treatment facility. That place was a joke to me; it was so transparent what they were doing and how they wanted patients to answer their stupid psychobabble questions. "A baboon could fool those assholes," I said to myself. I would take my mother's beatings any day over another night in that hospital.

What did change about me was that I got better at hiding my anorexia. I would eat just enough to make people happy, wear baggy clothes to hide my skinny frame, and lie about foods I had eaten with a smile on my face.

Mom didn't let up on me at all. Now that I was going on sixteen years old, Mom was tougher than ever. I was rarely allowed out of the house except to go to school, and I was never allowed out on weekend nights. No boyfriends, no football games, no sleepovers. "I'm not going to have my daughter knocked up at sixteen!" Mom would declare to anyone who would listen.

I desperately wanted a friend: someone to talk to, someone to confide in, a shoulder to cry on. I would sit in the house on Friday nights, listening to the sounds of the football game from down the street. I would hear the kids laughing, the cheerleaders yelling, the crowd roaring; and my heart would ache.

It was about a week until Homecoming during my sophmore year of high school l. I had never been to Homecoming and never even been asked before. Who would want to go with the shoplifting anorexic girl? My reputation at school was so tarnished that I felt I would never have a date.

"Sarah?"

I was in the school library, working on some math homework during study hall, when I heard a soft female voice in my ear. I looked up and was shocked to see one of the most popular girls in school, Susan, kneeling next to me with a smile on her face.

"Um . . . yeah. Hi!" I stammered nervously.

Susan brushed her fingers through her long, blonde hair and gestured toward the back of the library. "Do you know Brian Schulte?"

I turned around. I knew *of* Brian: he was in football and he was a junior. Other than in study hall, I never even saw him during the day. I strained my eyes to focus on the boy waving at me. Then I turned back to Susan, sure that I was being set up. "No, I don't know him; I know *of* him."

"He wants to know if you would go to Homecoming with him."

My heart raced and my face flushed. This was too good to be true; this had to be a prank. "Seriously?" I asked Susan, searching her face for any sign of betrayal.

Susan smiled again. "Seriously!" she exclaimed. "Well, would you at least meet him at lunch or something?" She was starting to get impatient and wanted to get back to her seat before the study hall monitor saw her.

"OK." The word was out of my mouth before I could even think. Susan slipped away, and I looked up at the clock. Thirty-six minutes until lunch. I drummed my fingers impatiently, fighting the urge to turn around and look at Brian.

Suddenly I heard Susan's laugh echoing in the back of the library, and my heart fell. "It's a trick! They're going to get me at lunch," I thought. "How could I have been so stupid?" I was ashamed of myself for falling into such an apparent trap, but what could I do? If I didn't show up at lunch, I would look like a coward. "Damn it!" I thought to myself. "I have to go, or they'll just get me after school—or tomorrow! Damn it!"

The next thirty-six minutes ticked away slowly, and each tick of the clock made my heart race faster and faster. Finally the bell rang, and I jumped up to gather my books. I wanted to get to the lunchroom first to assess the situation and find a seat by the door in case I wanted to run away.

Before I could walk out of the library, I felt a hand on my shoulder. I turned around, and there was Brian Schulte with a smile on his face. His face was flushed red, and upon closer look I could see that the redness wasn't heat, it was acne—and a lot of it. Brian was much shorter than me, and his hair was greased back—not exactly what I had pictured as my Prince Charming. But I looked at his eyes and immediately felt guilty for being judgmental. He had the kindest, brightest eyes I had ever seen, and his smile immediately put me at ease.

"Sarah, I'm so sorry! I told Susan that I would do it, but she didn't want to wait!"

"So this isn't a joke?" I asked hesitantly.

"God, no! I just like you and I thought I'd ask you to Homecoming. I'm just really shy, so Susan usually does all my dirty work!"

"Holy crap. This is for real!" I thought to myself. "Really? You're asking me to Homecoming?" I asked Brian with a hint of sarcasm in my voice.

"Well, Susan asked you officially," Brian said with a laugh.
"Um . . . yes!" I said excitedly.

Brian held out his hand and said, "So . . . do we shake on it or what?"

I grabbed his hand and shook it firmly. "It's a date!" I said.

My head was swimming. I had never been asked out on a date before, especially one as important as the Homecoming dance. I had given up all hopes of dating the moment everyone started calling me "Harvester" at school, but Brian didn't seem to care. "Maybe he doesn't know my reputation," I thought anxiously. But that was impossible. "He has to know—he's lived in this town longer than I have!"

For the rest of the day, I found it very hard to concentrate on anything but the upcoming dance. What was I going to wear? How was I going to do my hair? What kind of makeup could I wear? It wasn't until last period, about half an hour before the final bell rang, when it hit me. "Mom is never going to let me do this!" I said to myself. Immediately my stomach sank and tears welled up in my eyes. "She is never going to let me go!" I considered finding Brian after school and telling him to forget it, risking another blow to my reputation, but something inside me didn't want to throw up the white flag of surrender to my mother just yet.

When the final bell rang, I got up, gathered my books, and headed out the front doors toward home. I took the long way home that day, contemplating various scenarios that I could present to my mother: deals I could make in order to get this one night, this one special night. I was deep in thought when a car pulled up beside me.

"Hey—you need a lift?"

I looked up. It was Brian, driving his dad's rusted old pickup truck, holding the door open for me to jump in. All thoughts of Mom left my head as I hopped into the passenger seat and slammed the door. For the next five minutes, Brian and I talked as if we had known each other for years. We talked about the little town we lived in, our mutual friends, school, and our pets. For the first time in a long time, I was comfortable, relaxed, and felt good around one of my peers.

Unfortunately, that feeling vanished when Brian's truck squeaked to a stop in front of my house. "Here you go!" Brian said cheerfully. "We'll talk more about Homecoming tomorrow!"

I looked at him and didn't have the heart to tell him that my mom was never going to let me go. "Absolutely!" I said, quickly jumping out of the truck. Brian waved and honked as he pulled away.

I turned around and looked at the front door. There was Mom, peeking out from behind the curtain. I didn't want to go in. I didn't want to deal with the questions, the insults, and then the beating that was sure to come. I was half tempted to run down the road after Brian, but I quickly changed my mind when Mom opened the door.

"Come on in, Sarah!" she said sarcastically. She stood to the side and held the front door open for me to enter. I walked in, flinching slightly out of habit as I passed her, and sat down at the kitchen table, waiting for the tirade to begin. I didn't have to wait long. Mom slammed the door and whipped around at me. "What are you now? A little whore? He has to be at least sixteen if he's driving! What were you doing in his truck?"

I didn't even answer her. I knew that anything that came out of my mouth would just be thrown back in my face and twisted around.

Mom bent over and got very close to my face. Her eyes were filled with hatred, and the corner of her mouth was curled up into a sneer. "So you think you're a big girl now, RIGHT?" I covered my face with my hands, but Mom snatched them away. She grabbed my bottom lip and twisted it until I thought she was going to rip it off my face.

"Look at you—putting your nasty nigger lips all over some boy!" Mom let go of my lip and stepped back and crossed her arms. "Look at you—who the hell would want you?" Mom laughed and started picking apart my body, piece by piece. "Yeah, I'm sure all the boys want your beautiful thunder thighs and your bubble butt. Don't forget that you only have one kidney—fucking idiot!"

My eyes welled up, and tears streamed down my face. This only gave Mom more ammunition.

"I guess I should have expected it. Your FATHER was a piece of shit, and so are you!"

Mom kept ranting in my face, and I began to tune her out. The anger in my stomach grew, and I felt flushed. No longer did I hear my mother's rants and raves; I was seeing flashes of her indiscretions over the years. "How dare she call *me* a whore?" I thought angrily.

Suddenly I blinked, looked at my mother, and said, "You know, I could tell Richard anytime what you do." I locked eyes with my mother and, for the first time in my life, saw fear in her eyes. Mom opened her mouth as if she wanted to say something, but no words came out.

The silence in the kitchen was deafening as Mom and I stared at each other, each waiting for the other to react. I didn't have to wait long. Mom's astonishment with my sudden show of bravery quickly changed into a blinding rage.

"YOU BITCH!" Mom screamed. She lunged at me and dragged me off my chair. I cowered on the floor, folding myself into a ball as Mom's fists came at me over and over again. "I'll kill you! I'll kill you, you ungrateful piece of shit!"

I started pleading with her. "Mom, stop! STOP!" But my pleas were useless. Mom's fists continued to rain down upon my body.

Suddenly Mom stopped and stood up. She left me on the floor of the kitchen, walked into the bathroom, and slammed the door. I lay motionless, unsure whether I should go to my room or stay as close to the front door as possible in case I needed to run out of the house. My body was throbbing and already starting to bruise from the beating I had just received, and I wasn't sure how much more I could take this time.

I heard the bathroom door open, and I shut my eyes as my mother's footsteps came closer and closer. Mom bent over and pulled me to my feet by my hair. She whipped me around to face her and held up a small green bottle of Excedrin.

"Take it!" Mom said in a low voice.

"What?" I asked incredulously.

"End it. Take the bottle and get the hell out of my life."

Shocked, I started crying again. This was a side of Mom I was not prepared for. I knew how to deal with the beatings and the name-calling and other mental abuse, but this—taking a bottle of pills!—this was something I didn't know how to handle.

"I don't want to take the bottle, Mom," I said in a pleading voice.

"Sit down in the living room," Mom said to me.

Still crying, I walked into the living room and sat in the armchair closest to the front door. My survival instincts were telling me to run, but I was too afraid to do anything. Mom knelt down in front of me. She held up the bottle and unscrewed the childproof cap.

"Don't you know how much I hate you?" she asked in a calm voice. "Don't you see that no one wants you here, how miserable you make all of us?"

I wept harder. There were many times during my childhood when I'd felt that Mom could have killed me, but this was real. This was life and death staring me in the face, in the form of a little green bottle of Excedrin.

"TAKE THE FUCKING BOTTLE!" Mom screamed at me.

I held out my hand and took the bottle from Mom. She backed up and sat on the couch facing me. Then she leaned forward on her elbows and said, "No one loves you, Sarah. Just end it now!"

I shut my eyes, and my entire life up to that point flashed through my mind. I recalled the beatings, the belts, my animals, the boy's grave at the cemetery—everything that I had been put through—and it occurred to me that my mother might be right. It would be easier for everyone, including me, if I wasn't around.

I put the open Excedrin bottle to my lips and tipped my head back to swallow the pills. Just as they hit my lips, Mom stood up and smacked me on the side of the head. The bottle of pills fell to the floor, and I jumped out of my chair.

"I can't believe you were really going to do it! Jesus Christ—you ARE crazy! NUTSO! FREAK!"

I couldn't take it anymore. Less than five minutes ago Mom was pushing me to kill myself, and when I obeyed she called me crazy. All I could see was the front door, and I ran toward it. Mom reached out to grab me and ended up grabbing the back of my blouse. The blouse ripped off my body, and I was left standing at the front door in my jeans and bra. Mom threw the blouse down and shoved me out the front door.

"Stand on the street like the whore you are!" Mom slammed the door in my face and locked it.

So I was left outside in my bra and jeans as neighbors and people from school drove by and stared in amazement. I ran around the house and hid behind the garage, where no one could see me from the road. I sat on the ground with my back against the garage, gripping my knees to my chest and sobbing.

"Why?" I sobbed. "Why?" I couldn't utter any other words. The hurt from my mother's fists, my near suicide, and the show I'd just put on for the entire town in my underwear had crushed my soul. I felt defeated and broken down; life was no longer worth living in my eyes.

"I didn't even ask her if I could go to Homecoming," I remembered. For some reason this made me laugh out loud. "I just got a ride home from him, and that's what happened!" This made me laugh even harder.

For the next hour I sat behind the garage in my bra and jeans, laughing and crying at the same time. A passerby might have thought there was a crazy woman in the garage, but I didn't care. I needed some form of release, and right now this was all I had.

Shortly before Richard came home from work, Mom called me into the house. Not a word was spoken between the two of us as the table was set and dinner was laid out. After setting the table, I went downstairs to put on a new shirt. I looked at my reflection and saw that my back and sides were covered in red marks, with bruises already starting to form. But I didn't notice the marks as much as my stomach. "Ugh!" I thought to myself. "I need to lose some more weight!" Almost on cue, my stomach growled, and the pain made me smile. Once again the pain from Mom's beatings was replaced by this hunger pain, and it helped me forget what had happened just a couple of hours ago.

Richard came in the house, and I went upstairs. He looked at me and saw a bruise starting to form on my arm. "Jesus Christ, Nancy! What the hell did she do now? You can't touch her like that anymore!"

Mom stormed into the room and said, "Well, unless you want to be called Grandpa, you just keep your mouth shut and let me deal with her."

Richard shook his head and sat down for dinner, immediately changing the subject to a construction problem he had experienced during the day. Mom shot me a smirk and a glance as if to say, "Ha! I won!"

I looked away and said, "I'm not hungry. I just want to go to bed."

"Fine by me!" retorted Mom. "Maybe then we can have an enjoyable meal!"

I turned to go downstairs. Before I made it to my room, Mom announced, "Oh, and you're grounded for two weeks! You go to school, you come home, that's it!"

"Well, there goes Homecoming!" I thought to myself.

The next day, I had to break the news to Brian that I couldn't go to Homecoming. I felt silly telling a junior that I was grounded, so I made up a story about having to be out of town for a family event. I couldn't tell if Brian believed my story, but he was nice about it. Then we went our separate ways, never really talking to each other again.

Homecoming night came, and Mom opened all the doors and windows. While I sat at the kitchen table and wrote *I will not disrespect my mother* hundreds of times, the sounds of the Homecoming football game down the street filled my house. The more I wrote, the angrier I got. The more sounds I heard from the football game, the more defiant I felt. "This has to end!" I thought to myself. "I have to get out of here."

I made my decision that October night: I was going to find a way out of that house. I needed to take matters into my own hands. I truly felt it was only a matter of time before Mom killed me.

= Chapter 10 =

My last day

The Monday after Homecoming, I went to school ashamed of having to back out of my first Homecoming dance, but with a sense of purpose. After the Excedrin incident with Mom, I was determined to fight back and find a way out of that house. I had reached my breaking point. The years of mental and physical abuse, coupled with the Excedrin incident, had finally caught up to me. I had to make a choice: stay in the house and put up with Mom for the next couple of years or find a way out and leave that home and that town forever.

There was one teacher at my high school that I felt very comfortable with. Mrs. Bechtold, my English teacher, was always so kind and so sweet to me. Deep down, I thought she knew about the things my mother did to me and treated me with extra kindness because of them. "That's who I'll get advice from—Mrs. Bechtold," I thought to myself. "Mrs. Bechtold will know what to do."

For the rest of the day, I formulated my speech to Mrs. Bechtold. I would lay out the years of abuse, the horrible things Mom did to animals, and the recent Excedrin incident. "She has to help—there has to be someone who would take me in for a year or so until I graduate!" As I thought about the possibility of leaving home, my eyes filled with tears of happiness. "She *has* to help!"

The final bell rang at the end of the day, and I rushed to Mrs. Bechtold's room to catch her before she left. As I approached the door, I heard the sound of children's voices coming from the room. I paused with my hand on the door-knob and peeked through the window into the classroom.

There was Mrs. Bechtold, holding both of her young daughters on her lap. All three of them were laughing whole-heartedly together. As I observed the happy scene, a wave of sadness and guilt washed over me. "I can't butt into this," I thought. "I can't mess up what they have going."

I let go of the doorknob, turned, and walked away. I had no idea what to do now. I didn't trust any other teacher in the school and didn't have any family to speak of—none that would take me in, away from Mom and Richard. Mrs. Bechtold was my only hope, but I couldn't bring myself to bring sadness upon that happy family.

I walked out the side door of the high school and headed down the street toward home. As I neared the first corner, I heard a wolf whistle coming from behind me. Two thoughts crossed my mind: "That isn't directed toward me" and "If it is, someone's just making fun of me." I continued walking until I heard a male voice yell, "Hey! You in the jeans!"

"Damn!" I thought. I had to turn around now, if only to make this person stop yelling. I turned around and noticed that the voice was coming from a group of kids standing on the sidewalk across from the high school. I knew what kind of reputation these kids had, and in some cases it was worse than mine! These were the smokers, the potheads, the "troublemakers." If I were to hang out with these people, my mother would snap.

This thought made me smile, and I began making my way toward the group. I recognized all their faces, but I had never really talked to these kids before because I didn't want to destroy what might be left of my reputation. There was Billie Jo, Rita, Joelle, Ryan, Max, Gigi, and one man that I had never met before.

"Were you yelling at me?" I asked him.

The man smiled and flipped his hair back. "I've never met you before—I'm Matt."

I was immediately lovestruck. Matt was tall, obviously in his 20s, with shoulder-length brown hair and blue eyes. My face flushed. "I . . . I . . . I'm Sarah," I stammered.

Max laughed out loud. "She's fucking nervous!" he gloated to Matt. "Seriously, girl," Max said to me, "he's nothing to be nervous about."

I laughed and put my bookbag on the ground. For the next hour I stood on the sidewalk, laughing and joking with this crowd that I had never hung out with before. I was deep in a discussion with Billie Jo about Mountain Dew versus Coke when I heard Matt say, "Why is this car stopping next to us? Who is that bitch staring at us?"

I didn't even have to turn around. I knew it was Mom. I should have been home at least forty-five minutes ago, and Mom was out looking for me. "Sarah—do you know her?" Billie Jo asked.

I turned around. There was Mom, staring at me and drumming her fingers on the top of the steering wheel. "That's my Mom," I said in disgust.

"Well, what the fuck does she want?" Max demanded.

Without thinking, I said, "To drag me home and beat the shit out of me."

"Fuck that!" Max said. "You don't have to go with her. Fuck her! Stay here with us."

For the first time in my life, I felt strong against my mother. I stood on the sidewalk with all my new friends behind me, crossed my arms, and stared back at Mom. Mom gave me a look of shock. Instead of yelling and screaming at me as I expected, she peeled off down the street, leaving my friends and me in the dust.

"You can come over to my house," Matt whispered into my ear. The hairs on my neck stood up, and I immediately forgot about Mom.

"Hell, yeah!" Max exclaimed. "We're all going to Matt's house." Immediately Max started planning the games we were going to play, who was going to get the beer, and who had cigarettes. Having never touched a beer or a cigarette, I felt a rush of adrenaline flow through my entire body.

I had a choice. I could disassociate from these people, go home, and deal with whatever Mom had in store for me, or I could just not go home and have the first fun night of my life. I thought of the scene of Mrs. Bechtold and her daughters. Recalling how happy they were together made me even angrier at my mother. "Mom doesn't know who any of these people are, especially Matt. There is no way she'll know where I am!" I thought to myself.

My choice was clear: I would not be going home that night. Whatever lay in store for me the next day, I would deal with it then. But tonight I was going to live and not be hurt or hit by Mom. For some reason, this group of my peers made me feel safe, and I felt as if they understood me.

"Let's do this!" I exclaimed.

"Ride with me then, Sarah!" said Billie Jo. "We can go back to my house and get some things and get ready."

After exchanging a few quick good-byes and setting up a time to meet, Billie Jo and I got into Billie's black truck and took off toward her house. The music was cranked up loud when Billie started the engine, and she immediately turned it off. As soon as we had pulled away from the group on the sidewalk, Billie turned to me and said, "OK, what the hell is up with your mom?"

Not knowing whether to fully trust Billie Jo at that point, I leaned back and squinted at her. "What do you mean?" I inquired, trying to sound innocent.

"You know what I mean. Moms don't look at their kids like that. What is her problem?"

And at that moment, I opened up and let Billie Jo into my life. I didn't go into great detail, but I gave Billie a quick overview of some of the most horrible things Mom had done to me. As I recounted some of my experiences, Billie Jo started crying. "I am *so* sorry, Sarah!" she said. "My mom and I have problems, but she would never hit me or do things to me like that."

I wanted to cry along with Billie Jo, but I was afraid of looking like a victim, like I wasn't strong. "It is what it is," I said matter-of-factly.

"You are *not* going home tonight. You can hide out at my house if you want. My mom will let you!"

"We'll see. Thanks for the invite and listening. I really appreciate it." I was trying to divert Billie's attention. Although I would have loved to accept the invitation to stay at Billie Jo's, I was still nervous about what my mother could possibly do if I didn't come home that night. I didn't want to involve anyone in anything my mother started.

"You just let me know. Oh, here we are. Mom's not home, so we can get ready without her bugging us!" Billie Jo was talking a mile a minute as she hopped out of the truck and ran up to the front door.

I followed Billie inside and shut the door. I looked around Billie's house, assessing it to see if it was a place I would want to live. It was a lot messier than my house, but comfortable. There was a funny smell from an animal—I couldn't tell if it was a dog or a cat—but nothing a few candles or fragrance sprays couldn't fix. The butterflies in my stomach disappeared, and I became more at ease. "I could stay here for a little while if I had to," I thought to myself.

"Sarah! Want to borrow something?" Billie Jo was peeking her head around the corner of the bathroom. "Just go through the closet and try on whatever you think will fit!"

I spent the rest of the afternoon in Billie Jo's room, trying on little outfits, doing my hair, and putting on makeup for the first time. Not once did we speak of Mom or anything from my past. Billie Jo and I made fun of some of the girls at school, and we gossiped about teachers and boys.

"OK—let's go!" Billie Jo finally said. She picked up her little purse and went into the bathroom to grab her lipstick.

I stood up and took one final look in the mirror. A reflection of a young woman was staring back at me. My hair was curled and pinned up, my lips were stained red, and my eyes were rimmed with shimmery eyeliner. I had found an adorable little dress to wear, and the hem stopped right above my knees and flared out. I did a quick spin in front of the mirror and felt like the little girl from my childhood, spinning around in front of the mirror with a black towel on my head.

"Come on!" Billie Jo exclaimed as she ran to the front door.

I snapped out of my reverie and ran after Billie. We hopped into her truck and headed down the country roads to Matt's house.

Billie pulled into a small gravel driveway. It led to an enormous farmhouse out in an area of Walnut I didn't even know existed until that very moment. Max and Gigi were already there and were standing in the driveway, beers in hand, ready to greet us as we got out.

"Ready to drink?" Gigi gleefully asked me.

"Sure!" I said, trying to sound cool, but really I was dying on the inside. I had never tasted beer before and didn't want to look like a loser in front of my new friends. I glanced over at Billie Jo and saw her crack open the beer that Max had given her and immediately start drinking it.

"Why not?" I thought to myself. I cracked open my own beer and took a deep swig.

"Ugh!" I sputtered as I spit the beer out of my mouth. "What the hell is that?"

"Haven't you ever had beer before?" Max asked mockingly.

"Sure I have . . . just not that kind," I said, praying that they would drop the conversation.

"Bullshit! You don't drink. Girl, if you don't drink, then don't pretend you drink around us. It's cool—you don't have to drink!"

Billie Jo winked at me and said, "But there are so many things other than beer!" I laughed, even though I had no idea what other things Billie Jo was talking about.

The back door to the farmhouse opened, and I saw Matt come outside. My heart fluttered again, and the butterflies returned to my stomach. He walked right over to me and put his arm around my shoulder. "I'm glad you came. Did you get something to drink?" he asked.

"You don't want to know!" laughed Billie Jo.

Matt looked at me and asked, "Would you like a personal tour?" His eyes seemed to pierce right into mine, and I suddenly felt very hot.

"Sure," I managed to whisper.

Matt took my hand and started his tour. As we walked around the farm, hand in hand, and Matt explained what was around each corner, I grew more comfortable with him and this new environment. Matt's farm reminded me of our farm and everything I had loved about it. I loved how big the sky was, how the old barns creaked when the wind blew through them, and I thought how nice it was to have someone who liked me to share it with.

"He's so much older than me!" I thought to myself. But that thought was fleeting as I realized that this could be a home for me until I graduated. Just when I started to summon up the courage to ask Matt if I could crash there for the night, he stopped in the middle of the barn, turned me toward him, and pulled me close.

"I'm so sorry about what your mom is doing to you. If you need a place to stay for a while, you can stay here. No pressure to do anything."

My heart soared. I had found my way out! I had found my knight in shining armor to rescue me from the evil queen. My eyes filled up with tears, and I buried my face in Matt's shoulder.

"Thank you so much," I said softly. "You have no idea . . ."

"Don't think twice about it. Let's get back to everyone else," Matt said. He pulled away, grabbed my hand, and headed back to Billie Jo and the others.

After my talk with Matt, I finally relaxed and ended up having the best night of my life. My new friends and I spent the night playing card games, drinking a little bit, watching movies, and lying under the stars talking for what seemed like hours.

As I lay on the ground with my hands behind my head, gazing up at the stars, I thought of my mother. I thought about how angry she must be right now and how I had truly defied Mom for the first time in my life. I thought of Richard and wondered if he was worried about me or if he was just ignoring the situation while Mom ranted and raved all night. Then I thought of Emily and the hell she must be going through right now with Mom. When I thought of my sister, I became sad. "If I'm not there anymore, Mom will just start beating her up," I thought to myself.

I shut my eyes and took a deep breath. "Should I go home? Should I just suck it up and face the music?" I wondered. Who knew what lay in store for me the next day? I planned to go to school tomorrow, hitching a ride with Billie Jo. Would Mom be there? Would she be waiting for me at the door? I started to imagine seeing my mother at school and what she would do or say. Would Mom drag me home by the hair? Would anyone at school step up and save me?

"Hey, beautiful!"

I snapped out of my trance and looked up. Matt was kneeling next to me with a smile on his face. "You OK?" he asked.

Any thought I had of going home that night left my mind. Just hearing someone call me beautiful made me happy beyond belief. "I'm fine," I said as I got to my feet.

I followed Matt and Billie Jo across the yard into the house. "It's late," yawned Billie Jo. "You ready to crash?"

I looked nervously at Matt. As if he were reading my mind, he said, "Why don't you two take the spare bedroom? Everyone else is crashing in the living room."

I gave Matt a hug and followed Billie Jo into the bedroom. After we had washed up and changed into some T-shirts to sleep in, we lay in bed together and stared at the ceiling.

"You nervous about your Mom?" Billie asked.

"Yeah. I don't know what to expect tomorrow," I replied.

"We have your back. We won't let her get you!" Billie Jo said.

This declaration from Billie Jo made me feel better, although I found it a bit absurd and unrealistic. No one had ever been able to stop Mom! But I felt better knowing that people understood me and believed the stories I told about my mom. The knot in my stomach loosened a bit, and I was able to close my eyes and go to sleep.

"Sarah! Sarah!" I blinked and opened my eyes to see Billie Jo in my face. "We have to go to school! Here, just wear this shirt and your jeans." Billie Jo was talking a mile a minute as I sat up and rubbed the sleep out of my eyes. As I looked around the room, it occurred to me that I really hadn't gone home last night. I had run away, successfully! There were no problems, no police, no Mom. Maybe this really was it. I cheerfully bounced out of bed and ran a brush through my hair.

"Sarah, we have to leave in like five minutes to make it on time!" Billie Jo was running a curling iron through her hair and applying mascara at the same time.

"Jesus, let me get dressed!" I said. The next five minutes were a blur of clothes, makeup, and hairbrushes as Billie Jo and I frantically tried to make it out the door on time.

Just as we made it to the front door, it occurred to me that I hadn't thanked Matt for the place to crash and for being so nice to me. "I have to say good-bye to Matt!" I told Billie Jo.

"We don't have time, come on! I'll bring you back tonight!" Billie Jo said impatiently.

Billie Jo and I ran out to her truck and hopped in. Just as we were pulling out of the driveway, we heard a loud whistle. Matt had run out of the house and was sprinting toward the truck.

"No good-bye?" he yelled.

He got to the truck and walked up to my window. I rolled it down, and Matt leaned in and kissed me on the lips. "Come back tonight," he said. Without another word, he sprinted back up the driveway into the house.

Billie Jo looked over at me and grinned. "He really likes you. I've never seen him like this with anyone before," she said.

"I can't get over it!" I exclaimed. "What's he really like? Tell me stories."

So for the entire drive to school, Billie Jo chattered on and on about how she had met Matt, what kind of girls he had dated before, and any other information she found pertinent. I spent most of the ride doubled over in laughter as Billie Jo shared stories about Matt. By the time Billie Jo pulled into the school parking lot and shut off her engine, I had forgotten all about my mom or any repercussions I would face that day. I happily hopped out of the truck and then heard Billie Jo say,

"Whoa, the cops are here."

My heart fell and my legs started shaking. Billie Jo turned to me with a look of fear on her face. "Shit, what the hell is going on?"

I knew that the police were there for me. I knew my mom was going to do whatever she had to in order to control me and squash my new rebellious attitude. The thought of running away crossed my mind, but I knew my mother would expect me to do something like that. "I won't show her I'm weak!" I resolved.

"Find me after school," I said to Billie Jo. I slammed the passenger door on Billie's truck and marched through the parking lot into the front door of the school.

Just as I had expected, standing there waiting for me were Mom, a Bureau County sheriff, and the school principal. Mom was standing at the top of the steps with her arms crossed and a smirk on her face. I looked her right in the eyes, almost defiantly, and held her gaze.

"Sarah, where were you last night?" asked my principal.

Without breaking my gaze from my mother's eyes, I answered, "I don't think that's any of your business." I knew I sounded disrespectful, but at that point I didn't care. My mother had conned two people who should have been protecting me, my principal and a sheriff, into believing that I was a truant, a runaway, and that I should be punished. What did it matter what I said to these people now?

"What do you want done, Mrs. Burleton?" the sheriff asked Mom.

"I want her arrested. Teach her a lesson!" retorted Mom. She broke her gaze from mine to look directly at the sheriff.

The sheriff cocked his head and gave Mom a confused look. He said, "Why don't we just leave her here for the day, and you make sure she comes home after school?"

Mom shook her head defiantly. "NO! Absolutely not! She is a threat to me and my family. She is smoking, on drugs, and running away now. I want her OUT!"

I looked at Mom and shook my head. Now she was accusing her own daughter of being a drug addict and begging the police to arrest her. I wanted to rush up the stairs and hit Mom as hard as I could, to make her hurt like she always made me hurt. But I smartly chose to stand quietly as the sheriff walked toward me. "Put your hands behind your back," he ordered in a low voice.

A crowd of students had gathered behind Mom at the top of the stairs. I glanced up at their shocked faces and at Mom standing in front of them with her arms crossed and a look on her face that plainly said, "I won!" Then I couldn't bear to look anymore. I hung my head and allowed the sheriff to lead me out of the school to his patrol car.

After the sheriff had loaded me into the back of the patrol car and pulled away, he turned around and said, "Get a good look, because this will probably be the last time you see this place."

"What is that supposed to mean?" I demanded.

"You're probably headed to a foster home," he answered and then turned back around.

I sat back in my seat and leaned my head on the headrest. "Whatever happens, happens. Whatever it takes, I'll be OK if I don't have to live at home anymore," I thought to myself.

At this point, anything—even a foster home—would be better than living with that woman.

Not another word was spoken between the sheriff and me for the rest of the ride. We pulled up to the county jail, and the sheriff got me out of the back of his squad car and led me in. "Just sit in this holding cell until we figure out what to do with you," he ordered, taking off my handcuffs.

I was put into a holding cell that was used as a drunk tank on weekends. The walls were brown, the sink was rusted, and the cot looked as if it had years of urine stains on it. But even in this horrible environment, I was encouraged. It wasn't home; it wasn't Mom. At least here I wouldn't be beaten.

I sat on that urine-stained cot for what seemed like eight hours before the sheriff came back and opened the door. "Your father is here to collect you. Hope you stay out of trouble," he said as he stepped aside to let me out of the holding cell.

I smiled at him and shook his hand as I walked past. At the end of the hallway, I saw Richard waiting for me. "At least Mom isn't here," I said to myself.

Richard didn't say a word as I approached; he just turned on his heel and headed toward the front door. I followed with trepidation, and the closer I got to Richard's car, the more nervous I became. I didn't know what to expect, what was going to happen to me. I felt like a caged lion looking for a way out.

Richard got in and started the engine. I got into the passenger seat, pulled my legs up into my chest, and stared out the window to avoid any contact with Richard. My pulse was racing and I kept peeking at him out of the corner of my eye, waiting for a random punch or a tirade of insults to come at me.

"I'm in big trouble with your mother for getting you," Richard finally said.

"Why did you get me?" I asked.

"I don't want you in jail. It's not right," he said matter-of-factly.

For a moment, I felt sorry for Richard. I felt sorry that he had also been a victim of Mom's for so many years. I wondered what kind of hell he had been put through, and how he would feel if he knew about all of Mom's indiscretions. I thought of telling Richard right then and there about everything I knew and had witnessed Mom do, but then I remembered the last beating I'd gotten from that and decided against it. I had no idea what was going to happen when I walked through the door to the house, and I didn't want to add fuel to the fire just yet.

Not another word was spoken for the rest of the ride. We came to a stop in the driveway of the house, and Richard got out and scurried inside. I took a deep breath, swallowed, and followed him.

When I walked through the front door, Richard was already seated on the couch watching television. Mom was sitting across from him in the recliner, tapping her foot and glaring at me. Sitting at the top of the stairs were several garbage bags filled with my clothes and personal belongings.

"God damn you for coming back! GOD DAMN YOU!" Mom shouted.

Something inside me snapped. I thought of Matt, my other new friends, and the life I could have, and rage filled my body. I picked up one of the garbage bags and threw it out the front door.

"Why have me arrested? If you want me gone, LET ME LEAVE!" I screamed at Mom.

"You fucking piece of shit!" Mom yelled and jumped up out of the recliner. As she approached me, time seemed to slow down. I didn't duck and cover as I normally did; I stood my ground, with my fists balled up at my sides. Mom looked down at my hands and stopped in her tracks.

"Oh, big bad druggie Sarah is going to hit me now? OOOH, someone thinks she's strong!"

I didn't budge or blink. I wanted Mom to come at me, wanted her to take a swing at me, because I was ready to fight back.

"I'M A DRUGGIE!" I yelled. I saw Richard turn around on the couch to see what was going on. "Why don't you tell Richard what a WHORE you are?"

Richard stood up, and Mom shot him a piercing look. "Don't you dare listen to her, Richard. She's just trying to save her own selfish ass!"

I should have stopped; I should have left it at that, but I didn't want to. I was done hiding my mother's lies and being afraid. "The FS guy! The construction guy! The guy you bought the car from! The guy from the video store! COME ON!" I screamed back at my mother.

Richard's mouth dropped open, and I saw tears in his eyes. "Not once, Nancy, not once did I ever stray from you or even think of cheating on you for the twelve years we have been together," he said.

Mom just stood there and stared at him with a look of shock on her face. Richard looked at me, looked at Mom, and then turned around and went into the bedroom he and Mom shared and shut the door. I felt a rush of pride. I had finally done it! I had exposed Mom to Richard. I had put my fear aside and gotten Mom where it really hurt.

Mom turned back to me, and in one fell swoop she was punching me in the stomach. I doubled over in pain, and Mom knocked me to the ground.

"Fucking bitch, fucking mistake, I SHOULD HAVE ABORTED YOU!" Mom screamed in my face. She grabbed my throat and started choking me and banging my head into the floor over and over and over. Then Mom started crying, "I hate you so much! I hate you so much!" and her grip grew tighter around my throat.

I was struggling to breathe, struggling to get Mom's fingers off my neck, and trying to wriggle my way out from underneath her. I looked up at Mom's face and felt pure hatred pulsing through my veins. I had never seen Mom cry before, but here she was, sobbing over me as she choked me, trying to kill me and end the mistake she had made sixteen years ago.

My fists balled up. All the years of beatings and mental abuse had finally caught up to me. My fist came up and connected with Mom's jaw. Mom's grip loosened from my neck and she fell backwards, clutching her face and screaming.

"SHE'S CRAZY! OH, MY GOD, SHE'S GOING TO KILL ME! RICHARD!" Mom wouldn't stop screaming and clutching her jaw, her eyes wide with feigned terror as she stumbled backwards on the floor away from me.

I stood up and looked down at my mother writhing on the floor. I felt tempted to kick Mom in the sides and in the stomach and make her feel a taste of the pain she'd put me through my entire life, but then Richard came out of the bedroom.

"RICHARD! CALL THE POLICE!" Mom was still screaming.

I looked at Richard and pointed to the blood dripping down my neck from Mom's fingernails. "I have a lot more marks, and I will press charges," I said to Richard.

"Get out," Richard said. "We are done here."

I searched his face for understanding. "So you mean I can just leave, just like that?" I asked.

"Get out. It's what everyone wants," he replied rather calmly.

All of a sudden, I got scared: scared at the prospect of leaving home, scared of going through my senior year of high school without my parents, scared of being sick. But then I looked down at my mother again, and my mother stopped screaming for a moment, cleared her throat deeply, and spit at me.

"Do what he says. Get the fuck out of my life!" she said. She got up off the floor and screamed "GET OUT!" before tearing off to the bathroom and slamming the door.

That was all I needed. I shook my head and picked up the remaining trash bags from the top of the stairs. Then I heard a small voice behind me.

"Bye, Sarah."

I turned around and saw Emily standing there in her frilly pink nightgown, with a confused look on her face. I put the trash bags down and knelt before Emily.

"I love you, Emily, but I can't stay here anymore. I have to leave," I said quietly. Emily didn't say a word, but she threw her arms around my neck and kissed me on the cheek. Fighting back tears, I squeezed her tightly and then stood up.

"See you," I said to Emily as I hoisted the trash bags up into my arms.

I kicked the front screen door open and walked down to the street. Then I turned around and took one last look at my family's house. The years of abuse in that little house flashed through my head, and suddenly I wasn't scared of leaving anymore. I walked to Billie Jo's house that night with my head held high, anticipating the future.

"No regrets?" Billie Jo asked me later that evening.

"No regrets," I replied before I turned out the light.

Epilogue

That was the last time I ever stayed in the little house in Walnut. I ended up staying with Billie Jo for a couple of days, and then I moved in with Matt. Although he was much older than me, he provided me with a place to stay and was kind to me. I was never called in as a runaway again, and I didn't see Mom or Richard again for many years. It was as if I'd been thrown away and forgotten about by both of them, which at the time was just fine with me.

Mom and Richard ended up divorcing, and Richard got custody of Emily. Mom quickly remarried and got divorced and then remarried again, this time to one of the men she'd been cheating on Richard with.

I stayed with Matt until I graduated from high school. I realized that everyone expected me to drop out of high school, get pregnant, and get married to this much older man—but I promised myself I wasn't going to be a statistic. I was going to prove Mom wrong, try to be the best I could be, and succeed in areas of my life that she never did.

I graduated from high school in 1996 with a scholarship to a small business college. I broke up with Matt, moved out of his house, and moved to Central Illinois with some friends in the hopes of finding a better life than little Walnut had to offer. I got a job, put myself through college, and graduated magna cum laude with a Bachelor of Science degree in business. And, although finding a man was the last thing on my mind, I ended up meeting my future husband.

My husband, Aron, saved my life in so many ways. He cried with me as I relived my abusive childhood, reassured me and supported me when I fell back into my anorexic ways, and stayed up many nights keeping dinner warm while I was in school. He was the driving force behind my writing this book and sharing my story with others. Without his love and support over the years, I am not sure that I would have been able to accomplish so much in my life.

I kept in contact with Richard over the years, primarily to stay in touch with Emily and get updates on how she was doing, but I still harbored deep resentment toward Richard and kept him at a safe distance. As of today, our relationship doesn't go deeper than one or two phone calls a year, which is OK with me.

I didn't talk to Mom again until 2007—after Aron and I had our first child, Evan. I felt that it was important for my son's sake to give Mom the benefit of the doubt, see if she had changed, and allow her back into my life to be a grandmother. Aron had deep reservations about this, but he promised to support me. I just wanted to try. I was an adult now, and I thought maybe I could have a more positive relationship with Mom now that I was all grown up.

I will never forget seeing her for the first time in sixteen years that April day in 2007. When I opened my front door and laid eyes on her, I felt as if I were twelve years old again and she was in my face, beating and berating me. I wanted Mom to hug me that day and say she was sorry for everything she had done to me, but she didn't do either of those things. I remember sitting there the entire day, watching Mom and getting angrier every time I heard her laugh or saw her touch my son. I couldn't do it. It was too painful to have her around me and my family, too painful to just push everything aside and act as if I'd had a normal childhood.

So, after Mom and her new husband finally left our house that day, I decided to cut her off. I e-mailed her later that evening and told her that I couldn't get over what she had done to me. I explained that I had initially wanted to try to put the past behind me, but after seeing her, it was just too hard. This was the message I sent:

Dear Mom,
I have come to the conclusion that I cannot have you in my life anymore. I have come too far over the years getting over everything you did to me to go back to square one. You seem to have forgotten everything you put me through as a child, so let me remind you of some things.

Remember lashing me with a belt until I had welts—oh, wait a minute—you had Richard do that dirty work for you. Remember choking, scratching, beating, and hair-pulling? Remember mocking Emily at the dinner table until we were all in tears because she stuttered? Remember teaching me to shoplift and lie about your affairs? I could keep going—but what is the point? I can't tell you how good it feels to get this off my chest. It is too bad it has to be over e-mail because I need to tell this to your face and show you the scars I have on my body from your fingernails digging into me.

You were a terrible mother and you still are. You lied so much to me about everything in your life and in mine. I think you truly live in a fantasy world and you believe what you say! Richard said a few years ago that you are "a lot better than you used to be." What the hell does that mean? Does that mean you aren't hanging dead cats in a pantry anymore or shooting one of my animals to death with a BB gun? If that is the case—then BRAVO! Animals MAY be safe now.

I realize that by writing this e-mail—any relationship with you is done. I have accepted that—I have finally accepted the fact that I have never really been a part of the family and never will be, and it really is a load off my shoulders. And it isn't *all* your fault—I personally don't want anything to do with the family and I don't want Evan to be around someone who could hurt another human being so much.

I pray something or someone can bring you the happiness that has been lacking in your life all these years. I wish you would get the counseling you so desperately need—just so you could once and for all admit to what you did to me growing up and come to terms with whatever you went through in your life to make you the person you are. I've been in counseling and could probably use more. But you know what every priest and counselor and family member has told me? "Forgive her, but keep her away." I'm working on the forgiveness, but I'm not there yet. But I can keep you away. Face it— you were terrible to me, and what you considered in your mind as "punishment" was ABUSE, mental and physical. It wasn't right and I'm not going to pretend anymore that it was. Do you know that I can't remember a time during my childhood when you hugged me and told me you loved me? That's sad and you should be ashamed of yourself.

As far as Evan is concerned—his grandma lives far, far away and he won't see her again. He's young enough—he will forget you. I won't forget you—because I know what NOT to do as a parent and I have you to thank for that. He will grow up never experiencing the horrors and torture that you put me through as a child.

Good-bye once and for all,
Sarah (a.k.a. Anorexic Annie, Kidney Kate, Bubble Butt, Thunder Thighs, Nigger Lips, Bug Eyes, Loser, Bitch, etc.)

Mom's one-line response was this: God you are nuts.

I had spent many years feeling angry and playing the victim. I was angry at the world for not helping me, angry at God for making that woman my mother, and angry at everyone else who'd had a better childhood than I did. Every day I would see the scars on my arm from Mom's fingernails and rage would fill my body. I would spend nights crying on Aron's shoulder. I would spend Mother's Day starving myself out of guilt for not calling Mom. I would cry every birthday when I didn't get a birthday card in the mail from Mom.

I know it must sound silly, after everything Mom did to me, that I had feelings of guilt or expectations of love from her, but for a long time I still had hope. I needed a mom: someone to call for cooking advice, for housecleaning advice, and for help when I needed it. I felt ashamed and embarrassed when a holiday or my college graduation rolled around and no one in my family showed up or called to congratulate me.

I started to think I *was* the problem; maybe I was as bad as she had said for all those years.

Then I allowed Mom back into my life, ever so briefly—and I finally realized that I was never the problem and that she was never going to change or admit that she had done anything wrong. When I invited Mom back into my life, I was hoping that she was a new woman: the mom I had always wanted and dreamed of. But that was a pipe dream. Mom is never going to change because she doesn't *want* to change. I would like to think that she is so ashamed of what she did to me as a child that she has blocked it out and maybe really has forgotten everything she put me through, but my gut tells me that she remembers and thinks she was justified in everything she did.

I haven't spoken to Mom again since I made the decision that she was no longer welcome in my life or in my home. It was a hard decision, but the right one.

I still think of my mother every day. I think of her now with pity, not anger. I pity her for throwing away her life. I pity her for losing out on a relationship with her grandchildren. I pity her for being so sad and miserable that the only way she could deal with her feelings was to torture her own child. If my mother taught me anything, it was how *not* to parent and how *not* to live my life.

Writing that e-mail to Mom helped me release years of anger and hurt. Writing this book has continued the process, helping me to finally shut the door on that chapter in my life. I can move on now! I am a beautiful, strong woman, a mother and a wife. I am proud of what I overcame, what I have accomplished, and what is yet to come. The future looks bright!

Made in the USA
San Bernardino, CA
03 July 2019